The Concept of Man in the Bible

DIVISION OF THE SOCIETY OF ST. PAUL

alba house
STATEN ISLAND, N.Y. 10314

THE CONCEPT OF MAN IN THE BIBLE

ALBERT GELIN, S.S. David M. Murphy, translator

Original title: L'Homme selon la Bible,
published by Ligel, Paris.
Translated by Rev. David M. Murphy.

Nihil Obstat:
Wilfrid T. Craugh
Censor Deputatus

Imprimatur:
✝ Fulton J. Sheen
Rochester, N.Y. June 1, 1967

Library of Congress Catalog Card Number: 68 - 17767

Designed, printed and bound in the U.S.A. by the Pauline Fathers and Brothers of the Society of St. Paul at Staten Island, New York, as part of their communications apostolate.

ORIGINAL EDITOR'S FOREWORD

The pages which you are going to read had their origin in a series of nine lectures which Father Albert Gelin gave on "The Concept of Man in the Bible" during an institute conducted by the Christian Brothers.

A few days before he died, Father Gelin, on his sick-bed, went over the text. He had begun to put it in final form on the very first day of the lecture series: the reader will note how many passages preserve the animated manner and vibrant character which made Father Gelin such a popular lecturer.[1]

Father Gelin's friends often said that the scholarly exegete in him was always trying to become just the simple teacher; in these lectures he succeeded in making the transition most happily. The scholar became a spiritual guide, and the students, listening to their professor, discovered in him a man turned eagerly toward God and always ready to be a friend.

An original, private publication of these lectures provoked very lively interest. We hope that the present edition will extend their good effects even more widely.

What love of the Bible is to be found in these pages! And how well such warm and pleasant pedagogy succeeds in unveiling the Bible's intimate meaning!

---

1. It has seemed appropriate in this translation to preserve the personal tone which made the book so lively and attractive in the original French. *Trans.*

TRANSLATOR'S NOTE

The present translation has been made from *L'homme selon la Bible* by Albert Gelin, S.S., published by Ligel (Paris, 1962). Father Gelin was professor of Old Testament on the Faculté Catholique de Théologie at Lyon. Details of his life may be found in the memorial volume *A la Rencontre de Dieu*: *Mémorial Albert Gelin* (Le Puy: Mappus, 1961); the lengthy bibliography cited there testifies to the prolific output of this scholarly and admired Sulpician. He died in 1960 at age fifty-eight.

The majority of the scriptural quotations found in this translation are taken from the Revised Standard Version, used with the kind permission of the National Council of the Churches of Christ. However, Father Gelin's point rather frequently depends on the literal wording of the original Hebrew or Greek text; in these cases, either the translation of the Revised Standard Version has been altered somewhat where necessary, or a new translation has been made from the biblical languages. A comparison with the Revised Standard Version will indicate when this has been done.

In accordance with the increasingly common practice of biblical scholars in the English-speaking world, the spelling of biblical names and places follows the RSV. Biblical citations are also made according to the RSV. The reader will note that what the Douay-Rheims version calls the four books of Kings are called 1 and 2 Samuel and 1 and 2 Kings in the RSV. The numbering of the psalms in the RSV follows the Hebrew Bible, while the Douay-Rheims follows the Vulgate, according to the following schema:

Revised Standard Version	Douay-Rheims
1 - 8	1 - 8
9	9 - 10
10 - 112	11 - 113
113	114, 115
114, 115	116
116 - 145	117 - 146
146, 147	147
148 - 150	148 - 150

I wish to express my deep appreciation to the Very Rev. Joseph P. Brennan for his generous help in scriptural matters, to Franklin L. Kamp for reading the manuscript and making many helpful suggestions, and to Mr. and Mrs. Roger Dauvergne for their assistance with the French text.

This translation is dedicated, with deep respect and filial love, to my father.

Rev. David M. Murphy
St. Bernard's Seminary
Rochester, New York

TABLE OF CONTENTS

CHAPTER 1:

Concepts of Man's Nature from Genesis to Wisdom

In this first chapter we shall examine some concepts of man's nature which are found in the Bible. In fact, many concepts concerning man make their appearance there, and we must carefully distinguish the properly Hebraic thought from the Greek influences.

I HEBREW CONCEPT OF MAN'S NATURE

1. *One single psycho-physiological organism made up of two elements.*

The Hebrew Bible always presents us with one psycho-physiological organism made up of two elements:

the *nephesh* and the *basar.* [1]

a) The *nephesh* (the soul).

In the Bible, this word designates a very complex reality; the word "soul" does not give its exact connotation.

---

1. I beg the reader to excuse my use of Hebrew (and Greek) words. It would be impossible otherwise to deal adequately with our subject, since the meaning of these terms, as we shall see, does not coincide exactly with any English word. [For a summary of these words, see the Lexicon at the end of the book. The transliteration of the words is, as the scholar will recognize, a simplified one, meant to be intelligible to the reader who knows no Hebrew. *Trans.*]

The *nephesh* in its basic meaning, is the *throat*. Jonah, at the bottom of the sea, cries to Yahweh in anguish: "The waters closed in over my *nephesh*" (*Jon.* 2: 5). In other words, "I am choking, I cannot breathe any more, because I have 'had it' up to my neck!" By metonymy *nephesh* means the *breath,* the act of breathing.

From here the meaning shades over into *desire, appetite.* Examples: "A righteous man has regard for the *nephesh* (appetite) of his beast, but the mercy of the wicked is cruel" (*Prv.* 12: 10). "The *nephesh* (desire) of the treacherous is for violence" (*Prv.* 13: 2). We should not be surprised if, in the word *nephesh,* there is always a pathetic note.

In the Hebrew Bible, *nephesh* finally has the meaning of the living *self,* the living *being.* This is the case in:

Psalm 103: 1. "Bless the Lord, O my *nephesh.*" It is often translated "my soul," but perhaps it would be better to say "my being."

Psalm 84: 2. "My *nephesh* longs, yea, faints for the courts of the Lord." The reference is to a pilgrim who wishes to go to Jerusalem and who prepares himself beforehand by exciting his desire. "My being longs" (more exact than "my soul"). My being: that which is deepest within myself.

I Samuel 18: 1. "The *nephesh* (soul) of Jonathan was knit to the *nephesh* (soul) of David, and Jonathan loved him as his own *nephesh* (as his own being, as himself)."

Thus, the *nephesh* is the *same dynamic element as the living being.* It is the living being itself, the person. "Then the Lord God formed man of dust from the ground, and breathed into his nostrils the breath of life; and man became a *nephesh* (living being)" (*Gn.* 2: 7). When the sacred writer wished to say "a living person," he simply said "a *nephesh*"; thus, when in Genesis 12: 5 Abraham is shown journeying from the region of the East to Canaan, he is said to have with him some *"nephesh,"* i.e., some people, some persons.

But we must go on even further. The *nephesh* continues to exist in Sheol, [2] where man is completely enfeebled and reduced to a mere shadow of himself (cf. *Nm.* 6: 6); however, the *nephesh* of the inhabitants of Sheol is said to be "dead." The *nephesh,* which is the center of self-awareness, the center of unity of our life force, is the individual person animated by his basic dynamism. We must not forget that the Bible does not indulge in philosophy but rather gives us a concrete, existential view of life.

In conclusion, we can say that "my *nephesh*" (my being) could just as well be translated into English by the personal pronoun reinforced by "self" (which includes the note of insistence and even the touch of pride suggested by the expression).

b) The *basar* (the flesh).

The second component of man is the *basar* (the body, the flesh). The word "flesh" which we are using here must not be taken in a pejorative sense only in St. Paul, and even in his writings, not consistently. The Old Testament, when treating of earthly and fleshly realities, did not manifest that aversion which we find in Jansenism and before that in Montanism. The Lord, during the eighteen centuries of the Old Testament, taught us to value earthly realities and "the land of the living."

In Hebrew, the *basar* is the *concrete manifestation of the nephesh.* It is never conceived of independently of the *nephesh,* since the Hebrew always places before our eyes a well-integrated organism, which has both physical and spiritual aspects.

We come to know the *nephesh* through the *basar,* through the flesh. The various parts of the body are regarded, in a number of texts, as corresponding to various "faculties" relating to and recapitulating the *nephesh.* These "faculties" are merely the

---

2. Sheol is not hell. The latter includes the notion of punishment; in Sheol there is no punishment. It is a place of waiting, where the inhabitants wait for nothing, leading an enfeebled life.

basar (the body) concentrating the whole person for an instant, as illustrated by the following examples:

The *heart* is an element as important in the Old Testament as in the New. See, for example, Matthew 15: 19 (the evil thoughts coming from the heart . . .). The heart is practically the equivalent of the *nephesh,* but the *nephesh incarnate.* God sees what is in the heart, and the heart must not be a "heart of stone" (*Ez.* 36: 26), but a heart of flesh, i.e., a heart that can be penetrated. Jeremiah seems to have been the first to use the expression "the circumcision of the heart" to signify that the "foreskin," which keeps the heart from opening to Yahweh, must be removed (*Jer.* 4: 4).

The *loins* and the heart go together. "O Lord . . . who triest the loins and hearts" (*Jer.* 11: 20): Jeremiah again seems to have invented that expression. The loins stand for the faculty of inmost thoughts, sensibilities, and hidden desires.

The *liver* is the faculty of basic emotions. (It is like the French expression, "to stir up the bile," i.e., to fret.) "My liver is poured out in grief," says the Jeremiah of Lamentations (*Lam.* 2: 11), speaking of his anger.

Other elements of the body are also employed to indicate the whole person. Psalm 16 presents this ensemble of faculties: "I bless the Lord who gives me counsel; in the night also my *loins* instruct me . . . . Therefore my *heart* is glad and my *bowels* rejoice; my *flesh* (*basar*) also dwells secure" (16: 7-9). See Psalm 84 as well.

When Malachi says (2: 7), "Lips of a priest should guard knowledge," the personality of the priest is entirely concentrated and summed up in his lips, since his function is to be the one who speaks, the messenger of Yahweh. Likewise, in Psalm 35: 9-10, we read: "My *nephesh* (my being) shall rejoice in Yahweh . . . . All my bones shall say, 'O Lord, who is like thee?' "

The blood, the lips, the bones: all are so many "faculties" which can display the whole personality in concentrated fashion.

2. *The source of the stability of the 'nephesh-basar' composite: the 'ruah' (spirit).*

The next element that we shall consider is perhaps the most unfamiliar and the most interesting, the *ruah* (spirit). Without the *ruah* the psycho-physiological composite *nephesh-basar* would have no life and would be devoid of consistency. The *ruah* is a life force bestowed from above which keeps the living being alive. In Genesis 2: 7 we see God breathing, emitting a *ruah,* a breath, into the clay which he will shape. This *ruah* gives consistency to the man who has become a living *nephesh,* a living being made of molded clay.

In the Bible, sickness is presented as a loss of *ruah*; when we become ill, our spirit more or less departs from us — in the Bible's words, "we give up our spirit." Sickness is a state of imbalance, while the recovery of health implies that *ruah* fills us again, or, more exactly, that God "recharges" us with breath, his breath.

Among the Hebrews, between sickness and death there is only a question of degree; sickness is the beginning of death. Death is the almost total loss of *ruah,* of breath. We can say that at death the *nephesh* is emptied out to the greatest possible degree; it becomes only a sort of empty sack, which can no longer stand up. But in Sheol, the person does not experience a total disappearance of being — otherwise there could be no thought of the day-to-come, the resurrection. In Sheol we have life, but it is an attenuated life, life in a very feeble form. We have almost completely lost our vital energy; the "fat," happy life of those people upon whom the psalmist looks with jaundiced eye is no more (cf. *Ps.* 73).

Sleep is also loss of *ruah.* Psalm 104 speaks of the living creatures (men, animals) who are going to sleep; their spirit leaves them then (for animals, too, have *ruah*). But in the morning Yahweh sends his spirit upon all living beings, and they rise to their feet and stand up again (*Ps.* 104, 29-30).

3. *Reflections on the application of this view of man's constitution.*

a) The idea of resurrection in the Bible is conceived of in relation to this view of man's make-up. The book of Daniel is the first to affirm the fact of the resurrection. It was written in 165 B.C. and represents Jewish thought, the most "Jewish" thought even of this age: it is the "manifesto" of the Jewish "sages" of that time. The author who writes under the name of Daniel praises the martyrs; he himself is a prospective martyr. He asserts that the martyrs will be brought back to life to take their place in the Kingdom of God which will be established on earth, at Jerusalem. God will send them his *ruah,* which will make them stand upright (*qum*).

In Sheol, there exists those whom the Bible calls *refaïm,* the weak ones, the completely "empty" people; even so, they are still *nephesh* (the *nephesh met,* i.e., dead ones). Thanks to the persistence of the *nephesh* — even in a weakened condition — the Lord can fill it again with breath (*ruah*), can "recharge" it with his spirit. It is thus that the resurrection is envisioned; this concept of *nephesh,* imperfect though it may be, is the means of safeguarding the continuance of the person.

b) The concept of *ruah* is of primary importance. Claude Tresmontant has shown this very clearly. (See the list of Suggested Readings at the end of this chapter.) It is a concept which bears witness to the essential relationship of man: man has value as man precisely through his dependent relationship to God. He is always in God's hands. We have good reason indeed to thank God each morning for our life which he has preserved for us.

The *ruah* is the cause of the continuation of man's day-by-day existence, but it is also a divine force which makes man "moral," which makes heroes and saints. For example, Joshua appears (*Nm.* 27: 18) as a man "in whom is the spirit," a man of *ruah.* When Ezekiel (ch. 36) dreams of a "renewal" of man in the messianic age, he sees Yahweh infusing his *ruah* into him again (v. 27): "And I will put my *ruah* (= my own power, my ability) within you, and cause you to walk in my statutes." See also Psalm 51: 11, "Take not thy holy Spirit from me." The Messiah, Messiah-King and Messiah-Prophet, will himself also be full of *ruah*: "Behold my servant . . . . I have put my Spirit upon him" (*Is*. 42: 1; see also *Is*. 61: 1).

The concept of *ruah* includes, then, a "supernatural" aspect.

c) Finally, this view of man comes very close, under many aspects, to that of modern anthropology: the physical and the psychic are very closely united.

II THE GREEK INFLUENCE

1. *The book of Wisdom.*

The book of Wisdom was written between 100 and 50 B.C. at Alexandria. It must be remembered that that Egyptian city, founded by Alexander at the end of the fourth century B.C., was the new Athens of its time. There was a very active intellectual life there and a lively awareness of all the latest currents of thought. There was social life, but also much scholarly production: dictionaries, books of historical research, memoirs, editions of the great Greek tragedies, as well as works of literature.

A colony of 100,000 Jews lived in the midst of this Hellenistic culture. The Bible was translated into Greek (a version called the "Septuagint"). Here, too, the book of Wisdom was written, which is one of the outstanding works of a literature which can be regarded as "missionary."

2. *The concept of man in the book of Wisdom.*

The anonymous author of Wisdom treats above all of happiness and man's final destiny. This was a time when anthologies were very common.[3] The author of Wisdom had read the works of Plato in these anthologies, and, in particular, he had read the *Phaedo,* that great work of Plato which treats of the immortality of the soul.

The genius of Israel is a genius of assimilation; its providential character is to be a "filter" for all that humanity has discovered. At Alexandria during this era, the Jewish spirit was in the process of assimilating the Greek classical outlook,[4] and, because of this, the author of Wisdom has given us a view of man which does not correspond exactly with the Hebrew concept.

This concept of man's nature is a very simple one, of the sort which the Greeks had sought since the time of the Orphics. The Orphics were a religious sect which flourished most widely in the eighth and seventh centuries before Christ and which influenced Plato. For the Orphics, "the body is a tomb," a belief which is revealed in their pun, *soma sema* (*soma* — body, *sema* — tomb). We are far removed here from the Hebraic concept of the body seen as a manifestation of the soul. Among the Greeks, as will be seen also in Descartes, there is a dichotomy between the body and the soul, and the union of body and soul is regarded as only "extrinsic" ("as a horseman is joined to his horse").

The soul is all that counts. Wisdom attributes to the soul "a special importance, destiny of its own" (Larcher). The soul, to which the personality is linked, is weighed down by the body.

3. *Two texts of Wisdom.*

Two texts of Wisdom, 9: 15 and 8: 19-20, must be read at this point:

---

3. In fact, a number of Greek tragedies (those of Aeschylus, for example), are known to us only through anthologies compiled at Alexandria during this period.

4. On this question of the "assimilative" genius of the Jewish people, read *Les Scribes inspirés* of Dom Duesberg of Maredsous.

Wisdom 9: 15. "A perishable body weighs down the soul, and this earthly tent burdens the thoughtful mind."

In the other passage (8: 19-20) Solomon is presented as the speaker. He is the spokesman of the sages, since he has undergone every type of experience. The Solomon who speaks here is an extraordinary Solomon; this Solomon is put in opposition to Hellenistic wisdom. Solomon knows everything:

> For it is he who gave me unerring knowledge of what exists,
> to know the structure of the world and the activity of the elements;
> the beginning and end and middle of times,
> the alternations of the solstices and the changes of the seasons,
> the cycles of the year and the constellations of the stars,
> the natures of animals and the tempers of wild beasts,
> the powers of spirits and the reasonings of men,
> the varieties of plants and the virtues of roots [pharmacology!]
> (*Wis.* 7: 17-20)

He is the sage par excellence.

Here is a summary of his view of man (8: 19-20): "As a child I was by nature well-endowed" (i.e., well-formed, in the physical sense — the Greeks said this only of the body). "A good soul fell to my lot." Thus, he seems at first to give priority to the body, then corrects himself in v. 20: "or rather, being good, I entered an undefiled body." The "I," which is the subject here, in the Greek mind gives unity to the human being, and the personality is here linked with the soul. The author remains Jewish despite everything: he emphasizes the primacy of the soul and the fact that it is without stain.

4. *Conclusions from our analysis.*

a) The fact that this two-fold concept of man's nature exists (the Hebraic and that of the book of Wisdom) suggests the conclusion that the Bible does not have a single view of man:

there are two — and we have still not considered the concept of man to which the Greek version of the Bible bears witness. In fact, this version was made by assimilated Jews: would not their tendency in translating into Greek have been to simplify the Hebraic distinctions which we have seen and to portray man according to their own framework of ideas?

b) *Consequences of Wisdom's view of man, with reference to man's last end.* The thing that counts for the author is that, as soon as death comes (that death which is, after all, no accident), the soul goes toward God and is taken up by God (a kind of divine abduction); it is at peace, in the temple of God, in a state of love.[5]

But nothing is said about resurrection. We have not yet arrived at that stage of revelation. This doctrine, in its historical unfolding, did not follow a single, consistent path, but proceeded by fits and starts in several directions. For us, at this point, it is enough that Wisdom's view of man's nature does not contradict the idea of resurrection; it cannot contradict it, since it does not even refer to it.

As examples of the different lines of development of the idea of resurrection, we have, on the one hand, the scene in Daniel 12: 2 (165 B.C.), in which God "recharges" the *nephesh* of the martyrs with his *ruah* and makes them rise again, and, on the other hand, the conclusions of a Platonic anthropological outlook, according to which the soul will live fully only when freed from its bodily matrix.

---

5. As our liturgy of the Mass says, in the *refrigerium*. An analysis and further development of this idea are given by P. Grelot, "L'eschatologie de la Sagesse et les Apocalypses juives," in the work *A la Rencontre de Dieu*, Mémorial Albert Gelin (Le Puy: Mappus 1961) pp. 165-178. As a matter of fact, it seems that, despite its "Greek" terminology, the eschatology of the book of Wisdom does not differ in essentials from that of the "Jewish" apocalyptic outlook. *Original editor's note.*

III SURVEY OF THE CONCEPT OF MAN'S NATURE IN THE NEW TESTAMENT ERA

To understand the New Testament's concept of man's nature, I think that we must begin with the work of the Jewish philosopher and historian Josephus, who lived at the time when the New Testament was being written.

1. *Josephus' concept of man's nature.*

Josephus fought in the ill-fated war of liberation in 70 A.D. He published his two works, *The Antiquities of the Jews* and *The History of the Jewish War,* to make his people better known and as a defense of them. It is for this reason that he is often led to speak of the opinions current among the Jews of that time, and, in the first place, of his own opinion (he was a Pharisee).

His view of man represents a sort of compromise, an attempt to synthesize the two tendencies we have seen heretofore. This synthesis takes place after death, in the context of the individual's final destiny.

"Pure souls," he says, "continue to exist after death. They attain a very holy place in heaven." Note that this is completely consistent with the view of Wisdom, in the Hellenistic perspective of a blessed immortality. But he continues: "Here, at the time when the change of eras takes place (the great, long-awaited change, the eschatological age), the pure souls will again take possession of sanctified bodies." We see, then, how he "saves" the doctrine of the resurrection. This is probably the same point of view which is found in the Gospels and in Saint Paul.

2. *In the writings of the New Testament.*

I shall content myself with noting a few texts to stimulate your research:

Luke 16: 19-31. This is the account of the poor Lazarus and

the wicked rich man. Lazarus, after his death, lives on even without his body. He is "in the bosom of Abraham."

Luke 23: 43. This is Jesus' answer to the thief on the cross. "Today you will be with me in Paradise."

Philippians 1: 23. "My desire is to depart and be with Christ."

II Corinthians 5: 1-4, 6, 8. After death

> we have a building from God, a house not made with hands, eternal in the heavens. Here indeed we groan, and long to put on [6] our heavenly dwelling, so that by putting it on we may not be found naked. For while we are still in this tent, we sigh with anxiety; not that we would be unclothed, but that we would be further clothed, so that what is mortal may be swallowed up by life .... So we are always of good courage; we know that while we are at home in the body we are away from the Lord .... We would rather be away from the body and at home with the Lord.

Apocalypse 6: 9. The martyrs who are under the altar waiting for resurrection. They are not yet risen: therefore, there must be an intermediate state.

All these texts presuppose that the notion of "soul" has become more important. The old Hebraic concept of man's nature has undergone somewhat of a change: it has been re-thought from a Greek point of view. But this greater appreciation of the soul's worth has come about principally because the mystery of Christ has been taken into account. The Christian dead are "with Christ," awaiting the final resurrection which he has merited for us.

---

6. Note the 'theology of clothing' underlying this whole passage. On this point, see the notes and references of the Bible of Jerusalem.

SUGGESTED READINGS

Dhorme, P., *L'emploi métaphorique des noms de parties du corps en hébreu et en accadien,* Paris, 1923.

Guillet, Jacques, *Themes of the Bible,* Notre Dame, Indiana: Fides Publishers, 1960, (Ch. 7).

Jacob, Edmond, *Theology of the Old Testament,* New York: Harper and Row, 1958, (Part 2, ch. 3).

Mork, Dom Wulstan, O.S.B., *The Biblical Meaning of Man,* Milwaukee: Bruce, 1967.

Renckens, S.J., H., *Israel's Concept of the Beginning,* New York: Herder and Herder, 1964, (Ch. 1-3).

Stendahl, Krister, ed., *Immortality and Resurrection* (four essays by Oscar Cullmann and others), New York: Macmillan, 1965.

Tresmontant, Claude, *A Study of Hebrew Thought,* New York: Desclee Co., 1960.

Wright, G. E., *The Biblical Doctrine of Man in Society,* (Ecumenical Biblical Studies, no. 2), London: S.C.M. Press, 1954.

CHAPTER 2:

The Scriptural Theme of the "Image"

Man, as he is described in the Bible, is a cluster of relationships. The first of these is that which exists between himself and God. This relationship — which makes him what he is — appears strikingly in the theme of man as "image" of God.

I THE TEXTS

First of all, let us read the texts in which the theme of the image is most clearly expressed.[1]

1. *Genesis* 1: 26-27

God says, "Let us make man in our image, after our likeness."

"Let *us*": this plural is in no sense a remnant of polytheism — there is no remnant of polytheism in the P document! The plural indicates God deliberating with himself or perhaps in the supposed presence of the heavenly court.

---

1. Note that these texts all come from the "priestly" tradition (the P document, or Priestly Code). This priestly source is, in the Pentateuch, the most recent – not from the point of view of existence but of the fixing of the text in writing. There was a very ancient priestly tradition in Israel; priests and Levites were, after all, the ancient leaders of Israel. But the priestly source, in its written form, is a well-informed source, full of genealogies and dates, a source which was put in final written form in the sixth and fifth centuries.

"Let us make *man*": the word "man" is a common noun, almost with the sense of "let us make 'mankind.' "

"In our *image*": the word "image" is a translation of the Hebrew word *selem,* which designates a representation in the form of a statue. The prophet Amos uses the same term (5: 26), when he speaks ironically of the Israelites transporting the statues of strange gods (statue = *selem*). "Image" is, therefore, to be taken here in a very concrete sense.

"After our *likeness*": the word "likeness" is a translation of the Hebrew word *demut,* a more abstract term than *selem.* It is sometimes used in the Bible in a very concrete and material sense, as, for example, in II Kings 16: 10 ff. Here we are told that the Priest-King Ahaz, while visiting the king of Assyria, sees an altar which strikes him as very beautiful. He sends the measurements and a model (*demut*) to the priest Uriah in Jerusalem in order that this new altar may replace the traditional one in the Temple.

2. *Genesis* 5: 1, 3.

"When God created man, he made him in the likeness of God.... When Adam had lived a hundred and thirty years, he became the father of a son in his own likeness, after his image, and named him Seth."

Adam (= man) was created in the likeness (*demut*) of Elohim. And in his turn Adam fathered a son in his likeness, in his image. The image can be said to have been passed on; it is a permanent possession of mankind, which continues to exist even in sinful man.

3. *Genesis* 9: 6.

"Whoever sheds the blood of man, by man shall his blood be shed; for God made man in his own image."

After the flood, sin remained in the world, and especially murder, which is stressed here. Yahweh institutes blood-vengeance, and this statute represents progress in the conception of justice.

One day, when blood-vengeance becomes vendetta, and when men kill blindly to avenge not a death, but a simple injury, courts will be instituted, and there will be an attempt to regulate vengeance by the law of retaliation (*lex talionis*), "an eye for an eye, a tooth for a tooth" (i.e., it is forbidden to inflict a more serious injury than you have suffered).

In this text murder has been stigmatized and punished because of this "image" of God which is in every man. It perhaps seems a bit strange to us to see this theme of God's image recalled in such a very concrete context: man in the concrete, man existing in flesh and blood, is the image of God, and consequently God is concerned that no one shed his blood.

Summary:

Selem = a statue in general.

Demut = an image, corresponding to the Greek *eikon* (cf. ikon).

In the texts which we have read, we have been able to establish that man is looked upon as inviolable, whose privilege persists despite all the vicissitudes of his history: the fact of being an image of God is for man a permanent endowment.

II THE SIGNIFICANCE OF THIS THEME

1. *Man (represents) God.*

How can man "represent" God? We shall briefly outline two of the theories.

a) *Koelher's*[2] *theory.*

Koehler thinks that man is "image of God" because he "represents" him by his stature, his upright posture. The fact that man stands upright differentiates him from animals.

2. A German Protestant who has developed a good, brief theology of the Old Testament.

You have certainly noticed in the Bible how the sacred writers insist so strongly on the difference between man and animals. This is the significance of the parade of the animals in the most ancient account of creation (*Gn.* 2: 18 ff.). God makes every kind of animal file by man so that he can search among them for a companion who will be his exact complement, both physically and morally — and no such helpmate is found. This is to make us aware, by a story, of that horror of bestiality which the neighboring civilizations did not at all feel. Primitive men — according to certain pagan myths — had known a phase of bestiality, eating and mating with animals. In biblical literature the horror of bestiality continues to be expressed, as, v.g., in Leviticus 18: 23, when Yahweh gives a formal command in apodictic terms: "You shall not lie with any beast." This is the law which corresponds to the mythical narrative of Adam's search and sums up its message.

According to Koehler, then, man is God's image because of his upright stature. It is an attractive theory, and it reminds me of the verse of Ovid in his *Metamorphoses*, "He has given man a sublime stature; he has ordered him to look at heaven and direct his gaze toward the stars." This is a very beautiful expression of the dignity of man.

Certain strictures, however, can be imposed on Koelher's theory. It would be very strange if the likeness to God were thus presented, i.e., in reference to bodily stature, by a *priestly* tradition. The priestly tradition is the most anti-anthropomorphic, the most radically oriented towards an uncompromising affirmation of the spirituality of God. Thus, in this tradition, God intervenes in creation by his voice alone, i.e., under his most spiritual aspect. It would seem difficult to suppose that the author of P wished to say that man resembles God insofar as he is endowed with an upright stance: this would imply that God himself is seen in man, which is not the case.

Moreover, we should notice that God "created man in his own image . . . male and female he created them" (*Gn.* 1: 27). Now, we never see feminine attributes applied to God in the Bible; nowhere is it said that Yahweh had a wife (except in the heretical practice among the Jews at Elephantine in Egypt). The spouse of Yahweh is none other than the People of Israel.

b) *Edmond Jacob's theory.*[3]

Let us consider whether, instead of accepting Koelher's physical analogy of upright stature, it might not be more satisfactory to interpret the idea of God's likeness in man in the following way: man receives from God a *royal function,* a *delegation to be lord of the animal kingdom.* This is expressed in Genesis 1: 26: "Let us make man in our image, after our likeness; and let them have dominion . . . over every creeping thing."

This same idea is repeated in Psalm 8, which is the best commentary on the theme of the image. This psalm recalls that God is transcendent. He is presented as tolerating no equal; his majesty is spoken of, as well as his glory in the heights of heaven — admiration for the work of his hands is found throughout the whole psalm.[4] The author, having first of all set his sights on the transcendence of God, goes on to say:

What is man that thou art mindful of him,
and the son of man that thou dost care for him?
Yet thou hast made him little less than God [a 'divinity,' an elohim, i.e., practically speaking, an angel], and dost crown him with glory and honor.

---

3. Edmond Jacob, *Theology of the Old Testament* (New York: Harper and Row, 1958), p. 166 ff.

4. Is it possible that this psalm, like Psalm 134, was sung during a nocturnal festival at the Temple in Jerusalem? That would explain the verse, "When I look at thy heavens . . . the moon and the stars which thou hast established."

Thou hast given him dominion over the works of thy hands;
thou hast put all things under his feet,
all sheep and oxen,
and also the beasts of the field [i.e., wild animals],
the birds of the air, and the fish of the sea,
whatever passes along the paths of the sea.

This insistence has considerable significance: we see that the resemblance to God rests principally in the power of dominion over lower creatures.

In the book of Sirach we find more of the same. This book is a late one, but one which nonetheless bears good witness to tradition. Ben Sira is a man of tradition; the book is set about 200 years before Christ in a period of political tranquillity, when everything which had been said in Israel was being recalled with care, both that which had filtered into Israel from the international vein of wisdom literature as well as that from the sacral tradition of the priests and prophets. Note how Sirach speaks of the "image," referring, naturally enough, to the first chapter of Genesis:

The Lord created man out of earth,
and turned him back to it again....
He endowed them with strength like his own,
and made them in his own image.
He placed the fear of them in all living beings,
and granted them dominion over beasts and birds....
(*Sir.* 17: 1 ff.)

The animals are, of course, real animals, but this term in the Bible also symbolizes chaotic forces. The animals are *symbols of evil*. In Genesis 4: 7 God said to Cain: "If you do well, will you not be accepted? And if you do not do well, sin is couching at the door; its desire is for you, but you must master it." Evil is pictured as an animal in oriental literatures, and we have numerous examples of this in the Bible. In Psalm 74, for example, these monstrous beasts, symbols of evil and sin, are spoken of by name: Leviathan, Tannin (Dragon), and Nahash (Serpent). There exists a certain affinity between these beasts and the watery element, the chaos of the primeval sea, from which God drew the world (cf. the battle of the giants and the gods in Hesiod). Yahweh conquered these forces and imposed order on this chaos.

In the so-called apocalyptic works enemy forces are also portrayed as beasts. See, for example, the book of Daniel, as well as the Apocalypse of St. John (ch. 13-17 in particular), in which the beast with seven heads, which comes forth from the sea spouting blasphemies, is the enemy of God.

Man rules over the beasts, but he is also the conqueror of evil: he is, by his very nature, the imitator of God, ready to fight against evil. In the expression "image of God," there is consequently something like a call to arms, a dynamic invitation to action.

We must add here that this term does not indicate any proud ideal of a superman, for, to remain an "image," man must maintain his relationship with God and consequently keep his proper distance: the image is not identical with the source of the image. To think oneself identical with the image leads to a fall; this is the temptation of Nahash: "You will be like Elohim." For humanity, as well as for Israel, this lack of a sense of proportion is the great sin: for example, read the reproach addressed to the prince of Tyre (*Ez.* 28: 2).

Summary:

The original sense of this theme of the image of God: man in the concrete is in the likeness of God, not because he has an upright stature which differentiates him from the animals (Koelher), but because he receives a delegation from God which expresses itself in dominion over the beasts, over the dynamic universe, and over sin. This theme is an invitation for man to struggle, and at the same time, to keep his proper place in relation to God.

2. *Richness of this theme.*

I wish to treat two questions here:

a) First, is this theme the source of the moral imperative, found often in the Old Testament, which directs man to imitate God?

My immediate answer would be in the negative. In fact, the great moralists in the Bible were the Levites and the prophets; now, both Levites and prophets belong to the sacral tradition, in which the covenant was the central reality. In accordance with the covenant they taught that man (the man of Israel) must imitate God as a wife imitates her husband (cf. *Hos.* 2: 16-22). The moral imperative of imitation takes its origin precisely from the theme of the covenant and not from that of the image.

But, once having said this, I think that our question still leads us to some aspect of the truth. The moral imperative of imitation can be said to have been derived from the theme of the image, if we take the term "imitation" in a very broad sense: imitate God in his battle against evil, in his labor, and be the humble reproduction of God's activity. "My Father is working still, and I am working" (*Jn.* 5: 17). In Exodus 20: 11, the example of God working six days and resting on the seventh is presented for Israel's imitation. There is an allusion here to the account of the creation in Genesis 1, which permits us to say that we are close to the theme of the image. It is also possible that this idea of the image is found in the background of the texts which have a more humanistic origin and are in the sapiential tradition, i.e., which are not so close to the theme of the covenant.

b) Second question: is not the theme of the image the source of an eschatology of man?

This is an idea which has taken on much importance in recent years, because of current research into the theme of the mysterious "Son of Man."

Bentzen [5] was very concerned to show the roots of messianic

5. A Danish critic, who died some years ago.

hope in this figure of man as image of God. According to his theory, man as image of God, the man pictured in Psalm 8, for example, is the king of Israel; it is one of the king's functions to return to rule everything in the universe. But, Bentzen continues, there were other functions besides that of king: the function of priest (representative of the world), and the function of prophet (speaker to the world). Now, "man as image of God" probably recapitulates all these functions; only in the course of time were these diverse functions dissociated from one another in Israel, and Israel began to await the coming of one "Man" who would be king, another who would be priest, and yet another who would be prophet.

Such, according to Bentzen, is the background of the whole messianic expectation. The Son of Man in the book of Daniel will be a renewal of the ancient figure of man, image of God, in the primitive Paradise: the Son of Man in Daniel fights the animals (the same theme as before). We shall see that Christ will be victorious over the animals in the desert of temptation; in this respect he is the messianic Son of Man. In Romans 5: 15 Christ seems to be presented as this long-awaited Man, and Hebrews 2: 6 attributes a messianic sense to the Man of Psalm 8.

Without trying to say the last word on this matter, we shall only say that there is a possibility that this theme of the image is the source of a "messianization" of the Man.

III DEVELOPMENT OF THE THEME

Whatever the actual relationship may be between the moral imperative of imitation and messianism, the theme of the image experienced a development in two directions.

1. *To be "image of God" = to participate in his incorruptibility (Wisdom).*

We have mentioned that the book of Wisdom came into

existence in a Greek environment. The high value placed on the soul in this book will, therefore, come as no surprise. For the author of Wisdom, we are images of God first of all because of our soul; it is spiritual, immortal, and consequently participates in God's incorruptibility.

> For God created man for incorruption,
> and made him in the image of his own eternity,
> but through the devil's envy death entered the world,
> and those who belong to his party experience it.
>
> (*Wis.* 2: 23-24)

2. *To be "image of God" = to participate in Christ* (*St. Paul*).

In Christian thought, it is preeminently Christ who is

> the image of the invisible God,
> the first-born of all creation.
>
> (*Col.* 1: 15; cf. II *Cor.* 4: 4)

Christ is the new man, the new Adam, the first of a new series of men. In order to understand the famous hymn in Philippians (2: 6-11), I think that we must keep the theme of the two Adams before our eyes. Christ Jesus, says St. Paul,

> though he was in the form of God,
> did not count equality with God a thing to be grasped,
> but emptied himself, taking the form of a servant,
> being born in the likeness of men.
>
> And being found in human form
> he humbled himself and became obedient unto death,
> even death on a cross.
>
> Therefore God has highly exalted him
> and bestowed on him the name which is above every name,
> that at the name of Jesus [a new name]
> every knee should bow,

in heaven and on earth and under the earth,
and every tongue confess
that Jesus Christ is Lord,
to the glory of God the Father.

We must place the history of the first Adam in parallel with that of the second.

The first Adam was the image of God; he became arrogant and forgot that image does not imply equality with God but relationship with him, a delegation of power. Furthermore, he shattered that image by wishing to exalt himself and was cast forth from Paradise.

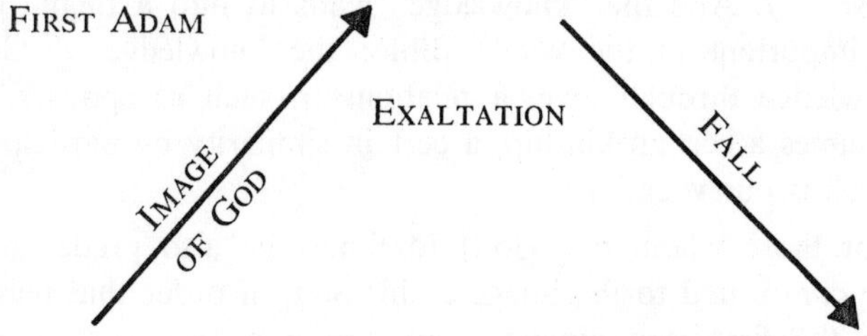

But Christ Jesus, the second Adam, did not exalt himself, on the ground of his likeness to God, but, on the contrary abased himself. This is why he was exalted and won us salvation.

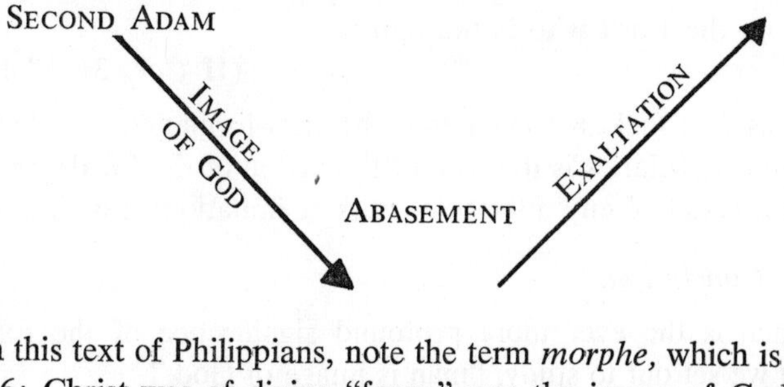

In this text of Philippians, note the term *morphe,* which is used in v. 6: Christ was of divine "form," was the image of God (by the very fact of his existence). The Hebrew words *selem* and *demut* were sometimes translated in the Septuagint by *eikon* and sometimes by *morphe*.

Not only is Christ, the new Adam, the perfect image of the transcendent God, but he has as his mission the transformation of us into images of that same God. For Christ is an image who is more than a "copy" of God. This subsisting image contains the properties of the original; it has the power to make us conform to the original. This is just what Paul means in his letter to the Colossians: "You have put . . . on the new nature, which is being renewed in knowledge after the image of its creator" (*Col.* 3: 9-10). The end of the verse is an allusion to Genesis 1: 26, which was our starting point. We "put on" Christ through baptism (cf. *Gal.* 3: 27). And the "knowledge" leads us into a theme which is so important in the whole Bible: the knowledge of God is a knowledge through love, a relationship such as spouses have; it presumes a certain kinship, a certain similarity by participation.

Such is our vocation:

> For those whom he [God] foreknew he also predestined to be conformed to the image of his Son, in order that he might be the first-born among many brethren.
>
> (*Rom.* 8: 29)

> Now the Lord is the Spirit . . . . And we all, with unveiled face, beholding the glory of the Lord, are being changed into his likeness from one degree of glory to another; for this comes from the Lord who is the Spirit.
>
> (II *Cor.* 3: 17-18)

This text makes it clear that the transformation of which we are the beneficiaries is the fruit of the action of the Lord Jesus and is not a result of any attempt of ours at imitation; it is "grace."

3. *Conclusion.*

Such is the ever more profound significance of the formula which we set out to study, "man is image of God."

In Genesis, man is image of God in the sense that he receives from God a delegation of power to rule over the world and to occupy a privileged place in the universe.

In Wisdom, man is image of God by his soul, spiritual and immortal.

In St. Paul, the state of image of God has been brought to us by Christ, in whom it is verified in the highest degree. It partakes of an eschatological nature, and we designate this ontological transformation, in abstract terms, by the expression "sanctifying grace." By clinging to Christ, the perfect image of God, we, in our turn, become "images," too.

SUGGESTED READINGS

Jacob, Edmond, *Theology of the Old Testament,* New York: Harper and Row, 1958, (Part 2, ch. 3). (The author, a Protestant, is professor of Old Testament on the theological faculty at Strasbourg.)

Prat, Fernand, *The Theology of St. Paul,* Westminster, Md.: Newman Press, 1958, (I, 310-322, 456-465).

Van Imschoot, Paul, *Theology of the Old Testament,* Vol. I: God, New York: Desclee Co., 1954.

CHAPTER 3:

The Human Couple in the Light of the Bible

Man, as seen in the Bible, is a network of relationships. Up to this point we have spoken principally of his relationship to God. We shall now consider man in his family situation.

I THE FAMILY AS BLESSING AND AS EDUCATIONAL MILIEU

Both of these themes are found in the Old Testament.

1. *The family as "blessing" of God.*

The first chapter of Genesis insists on this idea of fecundity. "God created man in his own image . . . male and female he created them. And God blessed them, and God said to them, 'Be fruitful and multiply, and fill the earth and subdue it' " (*Gn.* 1: 27-28).

The Old Testament is an economy of expectation, designed to assure the future existence and continuity of the People of God. Why is this idea of fecundity so important? It is because fecundity, i.e., numerous descendants, represents a "blessing of Yahweh" (blessing, in Hebrew = *beraka* [1]). The dominant idea,

1. *Beraka* comes from the root *berek,* which means "knee" (cf. the French word *baraquer,* which comes from the Arabic and means to make a camel kneel in order to load it). "Knee" is a euphemism – euphemisms are very common in Semitic languages – to designate the lap or the bosom of a woman.

then, at the institution of the human couple, is that of fecundity.

In the Old Testament, sanctions (reward or punishment) are essentially of an earthly order; it was reserved to the New Testament to complete the revelation of a heaven and hell in the world beyond. The blessing of God is the family, a numerous and happy family. Let us take note of what reinforces the "religious" aspect: God grants the blessing, God becomes involved in human life, God enables the woman to give birth. "I have gotten a man with the help of Yahweh" (*Gn.* 4: 1), cried our mother Eve after having given birth to Cain. And the name Jephthah means "God opens (the mother's womb)." The good wishes addressed to the young Rebekah as she is returning from her marriage testify to this theme of fecundity-blessing: "Our sister, be the mother of thousands of ten thousands; and may your descendants possess the gate of those who hate them!"

A certain number of other ideas in the Old Testament are connected with this theme.

a) *The theme of the sterile woman.*

Some of the patriarchs' wives, and the mothers of Samson, Samuel, and John the Baptist experienced this trial of sterility. The condition was a particularly catastrophic one for Abraham, since God had said to him, "I will make of you a great nation, and I will bless you, and make your name great, so that you will be a blessing" (*Gn.* 12: 2). And his wife had no offspring — she was sterile . . . .

All this is to make us understand that God controls procreation and reserves this blessing to himself. This is true even to the extent that in the Old Testament it is forbidden to conduct a census; in II Samuel 2: 24 we see David punished for having wished to violate this command. The reason for this prohibition is that no one has the right to interfere in God's own domain.

b) *The institution of the levirate.*

The levirate law was instituted to insure that a man would have descendants. When a man died without offspring, it was necessary to provide him with descendants; to accomplish this, his widow had to become the wife of his nearest relative (cf. *Dt.* 25: 5 ff.).

c) *The polygamous family.*

This is also the reason why families larger than ours are found in the Old Testament. Polygamy was readily practiced in the Old Testament. If the wife had no child, a concubine was obtained. The wives of the first rank themselves chose the concubine who would produce children in their place. You know the story of Abraham as well as the development which St. Paul gave it: the wife of the covenant, of the promise (Sarah) and the concubine (Hagar). And the patriarch Jacob had four wives, two of them concubines.

The polygamous family is further explained by the fact that sexual life was very disciplined. In the Old Testament sexual prohibitions or taboos are extremely numerous: [2] during his wife's pregnancy, the husband did not have the right to approach her; this was true also during her menstrual period, during the forty day period after giving birth (cf. *Ez.* 18: 6), as well as when the husband was leaving for war (a holy undertaking).

d) *The meaning of celibacy had not yet been discovered.*

For these same reasons, the observance of perfect chastity (like that of poverty) could not be injected into the Old Testament.

---

2. These prohibitions probably reach back to the origin of man, at which time it was found useful to have discipline on these two key points, food and sexuality. See our article "Interdits" in *Catholicisme* (Paris: Letouzey, 1948 – . . .).

Jeremiah is the only bachelor whom we meet in the Old Testament; he was celibate so that he might be a living symbol and might make the heedless understand the instability of their age: when everything is going badly a man does not start a family (cf. *Jer.* 16: 3-4). But in the Old Testament the command is "be fruitful." What is important, then, is to assure the survival and development of the People of God for the accomplishment of his plans. God's blessing consists precisely in this carnal fecundity, which is the result of his personal intervention.

2. *The family as educational milieu.*

However, it must be well understood that the family in the Old Testament is not defined only by the quantitative aspect, i.e., by the large number of offspring. The time even came when the sage (Ben Sira) gave this type of warning:

Do not desire a multitude of useless children,
  nor rejoice in ungodly sons.
If they multiply, do not rejoice in them,
  unless the fear of the Lord is in them . . . .
for one is better than a thousand,
  and to die childless is better than to have ungodly children.
(*Sir.* 16: 1-3)

If the people of Israel must be numerous, they must be, above all, of good quality. This presumes that the family should be the center of education — the only center of education. The Old Testament gives thorough directions on how to rear children.

The book of Proverbs restates a very old humanist outlook, which did not have its origin in Israel, but in the great cosmopolitan and cultured cities of ancient times, like Qiryat-Sepher in Canaan, for example, which means "City of the Book." A general moral system came into existence among these learned men of every nation, and they expressed its dictates in aphorisms. In the book of Proverbs, we often find maxims which are not exactly of holy origin, but which Israel knew how to assimilate to its religious ethic:

> Folly is bound up in the heart of a child,
> but the rod of discipline drives it far from him.[3]
> (*Prv.* 22: 15)
>
> Do not withhold discipline from a child;
> if you beat him with a rod, he will not die.
> (*Prv.* 23: 13)
>
> He who spares the rod hates his son,
> but he who loves him is diligent to discipline him.
> (*Prv.* 13: 24)

Deuteronomy shows how disrespectful it is for a child to mock his parents:

> If a man has a stubborn and rebellious son, he will not obey the voice of his father or the voice of his mother, and, though they chastise him, will not give heed to them, then his father and his mother shall take hold of him and bring him out to the elders of his city at the gate of the place where he lives, and they shall say to the elders of the city, "This our son is stubborn and rebellious, he will not obey our voice; he is a glutton and a drunkard." Then all the men of the city shall stone him to death with stones; so you shall purge the evil from your midst; and all Israel shall hear, and fear.
> (*Dt.* 21: 18-21)

These stoning incidents were not, of course, very numerous. Deuteronomy is a book which tries to point out an ideal, but this does not mean that everything it prescribed actually became customary. But we assert that the family is in fact the milieu which passes on the religious traditions to the children.

---

3. "Whack them on the backside – that's where their ears are," was an old Egyptian maxim.

The influence of the book of Proverbs was greatest after the Exile, when it became everybody's possession and did not remain only the book of a guild of sages. The book of Proverbs continually insists upon this theme of education by the father and the mother — and it turns out that the mother takes first place. We have here that very warm educational milieu which appears in the second book of Maccabees, where a mother teaches her seven sons not to fear death (II *Mc.* 7).

II IS THERE A MYSTIQUE OF THE COUPLE IN THE OLD TESTAMENT?

The account in the second chapter of Genesis emphasizes the idea of the intimacy of the couple: it treats of a couple united by love.

1. *The fundamental text* (*Gn.* 2: 18-24) *and its echoes.*

"Then the Lord God said, 'It is not good that the man should be alone; I will make him a helper fit for him' " (v. 18).

"Fit for him" = who is similar to himself, who is the physical and fleshly counterpart of man, but also a being who would be a help to him.

"So out of the ground the Lord God formed every beast of the field and every bird of the air, and brought them to the man to see what he would call them; and whatever the man called every living creature, that was its name" (v. 19). In the Bible, giving a name to a creature is the same as having the upper hand over it, taming it, or taking it into one's service or possession.

> The man gave names to all cattle, and to the birds of the air, and to every beast of the field; but for the man there was not found a helper fit for him. So the Lord God caused a deep sleep to fall upon the man, and while he slept took one of his ribs and closed up its place with flesh; and the rib which the

Lord God had taken from the man he made into a woman and brought her to the man. Then the man said,

"This at last is bone of my bones
  and flesh of my flesh;
she shall be called Woman,
  because she was taken out of Man."

(vv. 20-23)

In this first hymn to conjugal love, the expression "bone of my bones and flesh of my flesh" is the biblical counterpart of our superlative degree (just as, for example, "Canticle of Canticles" means "Best of Canticles"); it should be compared with the declaration of the tribes to David demanding that he be their king: "Behold, we are your bone and flesh" (II *Sm.* 5: 1). Between man and woman there is a supreme kinship, a perfect conformity. But in order that he might be given this woman, Adam must fall into a deep sleep, which resembles death. He must renounce himself to some extent and accept a type of death. The second half of v. 23 is a play on words in Hebrew: *ish* means man, and the one who is taken from man will be called *ishsha,* "woman."

"Therefore a man leaves his father and his mother and cleaves to his wife, and they become one flesh" (v. 24).

"One flesh" = one single being. The "prophet" — prophet of the past, so to speak — who wrote this account of Paradise presents the first couple to us in the poetic atmosphere of a new world inhabited by animals, from among which Adam will not take his partner. There is a counter-myth here, an apologetic passage directed against the Babylonian myth which recalled a stage of primitive bestiality.

The monogamous couple of the primeval age is presented, in v. 24, as a prototype for imitation by Israel. At the time when this was written, the author knew well what had become of this ideal. Still this did not keep him from presenting it as an ideal. The domineering attitude of man toward woman and the seductiveness of woman towards man are disorders and fruit of sin. Later, the prophet Malachi recalls this text on the ideal relationship of husband and wife, but he cannot call it to mind without bitterness, since he observes the manner in which, in his time, youthful marriages were breaking up.

> The Lord was witness to the covenant between you and the wife of your youth, to whom you have been faithless, though she is your companion and your wife by covenant. Has not the one God made and sustained for us the spirit of life? And what does he desire? Godly offspring. So take heed to yourselves, and let none be faithless to the wife of his youth. "For I hate divorce, says the Lord God of Israel . . . ."
>
> (*Mal.* 2: 14-16)

Thus the old text of Genesis 2: 18-24 is taken up again in an attempt to go more deeply into this mystique of the couple. References to this text are also found in Tobit 8: 6, Matthew 19: 5, and Ephesians 5: 31.

2. *The call of the bride and the bridegroom.*

The Canticle of Canticles introduces us into the world of love, into the very beginning of the betrothal, and into the atmosphere of the first days of a marriage.

This book is meant to refer, it seems, to a custom found in Israel and referred to by Jeremiah (25: 10): the saddest of all times will be when the sound of the millstone in the houses ceases and when the light is seen no longer and the calls of the lover and the beloved are heard no more. This call is precisely what re-echoes through the Canticle of Canticles: a hymn to the lost Paradise of a love as ideal as it was at the beginning. This book engages in sapiential reflection on the mystique of the couple which is presented in Genesis, chapter 2.

3. *The realistic warnings of Proverbs.*

In this sapiential book we must note the very realistic warnings formulated by the sages, especially in Proverbs 5: 15 ff. We find "the wife of your youth" mentioned there; the metaphors of this passage refer to the legitimate spouse (cf. the Canticle of Canticles):

Drink water from your own cistern,
flowing water from your own well.
Should your springs be scattered abroad,
streams of water in the streets?
Let them be for yourself alone,
and not for strangers with you.
Let your fountain be blessed,
and rejoice in the wife of your youth,
a lovely hind, a graceful doe.
Let her affection fill you at all times with delight,
be infatuated always with her love.
Why should you be infatuated, my son with a loose woman
and embrace the bosom of an adventuress?
(*Prv.* 5: 15-20)

This is a part of an all-out effort to inculcate the strictest monogamy. This monogamous ideal is also extolled in the song of praise to the "strong woman" (a better translation would be "ideal woman") in chapter 31 of the same book.[4] The perfect woman is a woman (one only) who has many children, who works and practices charity; she works at night, and during the day she cares for the needs of her family and servants; she ponders how to enrich her household; she does everything .... And her husband, at the gates of the city, heaps praise upon her:

"Many women have done excellently,
but you surpass them all."

4. This passage is an alphabetical acrostic poem: the first letters of each verse taken together, make up the Hebrew alphabet. This results in a type of poem which necessarily has a slightly diffuse and artificial character.

Charm is deceitful, and beauty is vain,
but a woman who fears the Lord is to be praised.[5]
(*Prv.* 31: 29-30)

Chapter 26 of Sirach persents the recollections of a sage who brings us right into his happy home; it is a monogamous home. He could not tolerate in his home the presence of two women who felt jealousy for each other:

A wife's charm delights her husband,
and her skill puts fat on his bones.
A silent wife is a gift of the Lord,
and there is nothing so precious as a disciplined soul.
A modest wife adds charm to charm,
and no balance can weigh the value of a chaste soul.
Like the sun rising in the heights of the Lord,
so is the beauty of a good wife in her well-ordered home.
(*Sir.* 26: 13-16)

4. *The circles of the sacral tradition.*

The sapiential milieu (from which Proverbs, Sirach, Deuteronomy, etc., have come) is not the only one which has to do with this question. The prophets, who, along with the Levites, constitute the "sacral" tradition, have set in relief a symbolism which is destined to have a very great influence: marriage will serve to express the relationship between Yahweh and Israel.

Hosea seems to have been the one to initiate this theme, which sprang from his own experience. The book of Hosea is an impassioned book, and that passion was given him as a sign from Yahweh to express the reality of the covenant through his marriage. In this marriage, the spouses are not on an equal spiritual

5. Father Gelin's opinion is that both of these verses were spoken by the husband and not the first one only, as the Revised Standard Version would have it. *Trans.*

level; this situation will help the prophet understand the gratuitous love of Yahweh for Israel: "Behold," says Yahweh, "I will allure her, and bring her into the wilderness [i.e., a quiet place] and speak tenderly to her" (*Hos.* 2: 14).

Israel is called the "vineyard of Yahweh" at the beginning of Isaiah, chapter 5:

> My beloved had a vineyard
> on a very fertile hill.

(Vineyard is a metaphorical expression for "wife." See the Canticle of Canticles.)

The same symbolism of betrothal and marriage is found in Jeremiah. Yahweh speaks to Jerusalem:

> I remember the devotion of your youth,
> your love as a bride,
> how you followed me in the wilderness,
> in a land not sown.
>
> (*Jer.* 2: 2)
>
> You have played the harlot with many lovers . . . .
> Where have you not been lain with?
> By the waysides you have set awaiting lovers
> like an Arab in the wilderness.
> You have polluted the land
> with your vile harlotry.
>
> (*Jer.* 3: 1-2)

In this vein the most moving text is unquestionably chapter 16 of Ezekiel:

> "As for your birth, on the day you were born your navel string was not cut, nor were you washed with water to cleanse you, nor rubbed with salt, nor swathed with bands. No eye pitied you, to do any of these things to you out of compassion for you; but you were cast out on the open field, for you were abhorred, on the day that you were born.

> "And when I passed by you, and saw you weltering in your blood, I said to you in your blood, 'Live, and grow up like a plant of the field.' And you grew up and became tall and arrived at full maidenhood; your breasts were formed, and your hair had grown; yet you were naked and bare. When I passed by you again and looked upon you, behold, you were at the age for love; and I spread my skirt over you, and covered your nakedness: yea, I plighted my troth to you and entered into a covenant with you, says the Lord God, and you became mine . . . ."
>
> (*Ez.* 16: 4-8)

We should next read Isaiah 54: 5 ff. — Second Isaiah, which was written during the Exile:

> For your Maker [O Jerusalem] is your husband,
> the Lord of hosts is his name;
> and the Holy One of Israel is your Redeemer,
> the God of the whole earth he is called.
> For the Lord has called you
> like a wife forsaken and grieved in spirit,
> like a wife of youth when she is cast off,
> says your God.

This theme of the Yahweh-Israel marriage is very important; one day St. Paul will transpose it as he speaks of the Christ-Church marriage. In order that marriage might be a fitting symbol of the Yahweh-Israel relationship, it is necessary that it already be a consecrated reality, but in return it receives an increase of religious dignity precisely because it has served as this symbol. The result of this is a progressive refinement in the field of morals, progress in the ideal of fidelity and monogamy — for Yahweh has only one spouse, Israel.

It is desirable here to point out some examples of marriages in keeping with these requirements, which become increasingly better understood. To continue with the book of Ezekiel, one can see there, in chapter 24: 15 ff., in what tender terms this tough prophet (Ezekiel means "God strengthens") speaks of his wife who is about to die: she is "the joy of his eyes." The marriage of Tobit is also one of the marriages in the Old Testament which appears to be a complete success. In this regard the fundamental text of Genesis 2: 18 is recalled: "And now, O Lord," prays Tobit, "I am not taking this sister of mine because of lust, but with sincerity. Grant that I may find mercy and may grow old together with her" (*Tb.* 8: 7).

5. *Legal steps against the plague of divorce.*

In addition to this campaign in favor of monogamy, Israel's legislative efforts themselves strove toward this end. The very important text of Deuteronomy 24: 1-4 on divorce should probably be placed in the seventh century before Christ.

This regulation on divorce brought about very great progress in family morality in Israel. To understand this seeming paradox, we must go beyond appearances. We have already had occasion to explain how the *lex talionis* represented immense progress in the realm of justice, since it replaced the vendetta, which was practiced without any hint of proportion between the crime committed and the injury inflicted in return. The same is true with the law of divorce; it puts some limit on a man's weakness, indulgence, and arbitrary will. It required a notice of repudiation; thus, the husband had to take time to reflect instead of dismissing his wife on the spur of the moment. This notice had to be presented to a court of elders. Although we do not know exactly what causes were judged sufficient, it is certain that a serious cause was required to take such a step. Finally, the husband was forbidden to take his wife back.

> When a man takes a wife and marries her, if then she finds no favor in his eyes because he has found some indecency in her, and he writes her a bill of divorce and puts it in her hand and sends her out of his house, and she departs out of

his house, and if she goes and becomes another man's wife, and the latter husband dislikes her and writes her a bill of divorce and puts it in her hand and sends her out of his house, or if the latter husband dies, who took her to be his wife, then her former husband, who sent her away, may not take her again to be his wife, after she has been defiled.[6]

(*Dt.* 24, 1-4)

The very law of divorce, seen as a restraining influence, therefore finds a place in our consideration of the mystique of the couple. Thus, in the Old Testament, progress is made from the theme of fecundity to an appreciation of the value of the couple who are characterized by love. This last point, however, will receive its full development in the New Testament.

III THE NEW TESTAMENT

The New Testament puts forward the ideal of a consecrated celibacy and, at the same time, raises the mystique of the couple to unsuspected heights.

1. *Consecrated celibacy.*

"Not all men can receive this precept, but only those to whom it is given. For there are eunuchs who have been so from birth, and there are eunuchs who have been made eunuchs by men, and there are eunuchs who have made themselves eunuchs for the sake of the kingdom of heaven" (*Mt.* 19: 11-12).

This celibacy is "consecrated," since it is "for the sake of the kingdom of heaven." This is why celibacy is always a mystery and a service, and consequently does not imply any egotistical withdrawal into oneself.

---

6. The word "defiled" does not in the least indicate any fault. It is a technical expression.

2. *Indissoluble marriage and the ideal of the couple.*

This same passage of Matthew takes up — as we have seen again and again — the text of Genesis 2: 18-24. Jesus, after recalling it, adds, "What therefore God has joined together, let no man put asunder" (*Mt.* 19: 6). And in response to a question of the Pharisees about the law of divorce, he replies, "For your hardness of heart Moses allowed you to divorce your wives, but from the beginning it was not so" (*Mt.* 19: 8).

We have, therefore, verified the fact that throughout the whole of the Bible this same primeval text has been taken up again with ever deeper insight. Jesus — like Jeremiah — was celibate and at the same time gave proof of a deep understanding and tender appreciation of family intimacy. It would be good if we could see Jesus in his years at Nazareth, during which he was brought up by two people who loved each other; it would be good to be able to observe the obedience of those years, the pride and upset of his parents on the occasion of his messianic adventure at twelve years of age, the marriage feast of Cana, the welcome Jesus was given by friendly families, the entreaties of Jairus for his sick little daughter, the tears of the widow of Nain, the words of Jesus concerning the children (no one spoke in such terms of children) .... All these concrete details show that Jesus had an inborn family sense. We are convinced of this when we hear him speaking of the father of a family who knows how to treat his children with kindness — bread and not a stone, an egg and not a scorpion .... We must listen to him speaking of the joy of a woman going to have a baby .... He insists on these details to teach us that we must create grandeur and love from them.

3. *The mystique of the couple in St. Paul.*

Here we reach a high peak with the text of Ephesians 5: 21-32:

> Be subject to one another out of reverence for Christ.

> Wives, be subject to your husbands, as to the Lord. For the husband is the head of the wife as Christ is the head of the church, his body, and is himself its Savior. As the church is subject to Christ, so let wives also be subject in everything to their husbands.
>
> Husbands, love your wives, as Christ loved the church and gave himself up for her, that he might sanctify her, having cleansed her by the washing of water with the word, that he might present the church to himself in splendor, without spot or wrinkle or any such thing, that she might be holy and without blemish. Even so husbands should love their wives as their own bodies. He who loves his wife loves himself. For no man ever hates his own flesh, but nourishes and cherishes it, as Christ does the church, because we are members of his body. "For this reason a man shall leave his father and mother and be joined to his wife, and the two shall become one" [*Gen.* 2: 24]. This is a great mystery, and I take it to mean Christ and the church.

When St. Paul urges Christian spouses to fulfill their duty, he invokes — as did Malachi and Tobit and Jesus — the ancient maxim on the ideal couple.

This is Christian marriage, but it is something else, too. An astounding parallel is proposed to a man and his wife: they must imitate the mutual relationship between Christ and the Church. In olden days the prophets had said: Yahweh loves Israel as a husband loves his wife — and to translate the word "love" into Greek, the word *"agape,"* which means love-gift, was used instead of *"eros,"* which corresponds to the love in which we are the beneficiaries. Christian conjugal love is a self-sacrificing love, following the example of Christ, who gave his life because he loved (cf. *Jn.* 10: 11; 13: 1). Christian marriage must, therefore, "imitate" the mutual relationship between Christ and the Church. But, as we have already emphasized in our previous explanations, in St. Paul "to imitate" does not mean that the person himself produces a copy on his own initiative, but it means "to participate in"; for the Christ-Church marriage (like that of Yahweh-Israel in former days) is not only the model but also the source of the relationship of the spouses. The Christ-Church mystery is not only given as an exemplary reality to contemplate, but as a grace to be shared. The conjugal state, therefore, has been radically renewed and given new value; in Christ and the Church, this relationship flourishes in love, in *agape*. The consecration of the man to the woman and the woman to the man consists in looking upon the spouses as an absolute, and he or she can only be regarded as such because there is, in the background, Christ and the Church. St. Paul was right to call this a "mystery" of great importance, because in it we are exposed to a transcendent world and the spouses must yield to a divine dimension. This, then, is what the sacrament of marriage, after Christ, brings to Christians.

SUGGESTED READINGS

Bonsirven, *Le divorce dans le N. T.*, Paris: Desclée and Co.

This remarkable little book clarifies a difficult passage in Matthew's Gospel (19: 9): "Whoever divorces his wife, except for unchastity, and marries another, commits adultery." It would seem that Christ allows one case in which it is permitted to divorce one's wife. Father Bonsirven remarks that the word *"fornication"* is used in French translations[7] as a translation of the Greek word *"porneia,"* which in turn corresponds to the Hebrew word *"zenut."* The word *"zenut"* refers to unions not recognized by the law, e.g., those without a proper contract, or those forbidden by kinship. Jesus (in the Gosepl of St. Matthew, i.e., in a Jewish context), therefore, wishes to say that he is making no mention of those unions which are not considered true marriages. He treats only of the legitimate wife – this goes without saying – and does not consider pseudo-marriages, for which the Jewish law iteslf had provided "divorce." Thus, *zenut* (= *porneia* = fornication) does not mean "prostitution," but rather "forbidden by law," i.e., in today's terminology, "directed impediments" (cf. the same term in *Acts* 15: 20, 29).

Dupont, Dom J., *Mariage et divorce dans l'Évangile* (Desclée de Brouwer).

Dom Dupont questions Bonsirven's solution, without offering a definitive one of his own. See *Revue Biblique,* 1960, pp. 463-464.

Gelin, Albert, "Le rôle de la famille dans la sanctification de l'humanité" in *L'Ami du Clergé,* 1952, pp. 545-551.

Grelot, Pierre, *Man and Wife in Scripture,* New York: Herder and Herder, 1964.

Leon-Dufour, Xavier, ed., *Vocabulaire de théologie biblique,* Paris: Les Éditions du Cerf, 1964, (Article "Mariage").

---

7. In English translations we find "unchastity" (Revised Standard Version), "fornication" (Douay-Rheims), "immorality" (Confraternity), and "unfaithfulness" (Knox). *Trans.*

CHAPTER 4:

Man Under the Covenant: The "Individual-Community" Tension

As we have said, the biblical man is defined by his relationships. We are now going to study his community ties and the manner in which immersion in a group harmonizes with personal autonomy and responsibility.

I THE FACT OF THIS TENSION: BASIC PRINCIPLES OF INTERPRETATION

1. *A certain dissonance.*

In the course of studying man in the Bible, it is impossible not to be aware of a certain dissonance.

a) On the one hand, the reader is struck by the *individuality of man.* He is "the one whom Yahweh has known" (*Ex.* 33: 17; *Jer.* 1: 5); see also Psalm 139: 1 ff.:

O Lord, thou hast searched me and known me!
Thou knowest when I sit down and when I rise up;
thou discernest my thoughts from afar . . . .

"To know" does not consist here in a superficial operation of the intellect, but an operation which involves and demands an intimacy. God pursues us, encounters us, cherishes us with his love. He takes the initiative in this knowledge through intimacy:

"Now that you have come to know God, or rather to be known by God . . ." (*Gal.* 4: 9).

The biblical man is he who is aware of this love of God pursuing him.

> What is man that thou art mindful of him,
> and the son of man that thou dost care for him?
> (*Ps.* 8: 4)

And St. Paul will speak to us of "the Son of God, who loved me and gave himself for me" (*Gal.* 2: 20).

An example of this appreciation of man as an individual can be found in the names which are called "theophoric names," i.e., those which are compounds of the name of God. These names manifest this consciousness of an individualistic piety, which sees in each man not only an object of God's activity but also an "I" face to face with a "YOU." A consciousness of the individual's spiritual uniqueness finds its expression in these ancient names. "Personal names," says Noth, who has studied them, "will always prove those wrong who maintain that they find in ancient times a relationship of divinity exclusively to the group." Some examples of these names:

Yeho-yada: God knows (as in our name "Theodore," which means "gift of God"), cf. II *Sm.* 8: 18;

Pada-yah: Yahweh redeems;

Elisha: God helps.

Many of these names were made up without any reference to a previous usage in Israel or in neighboring lands.

b) At the same time, man appears to us *immersed in a group*. It could be said that God pays more attention to this group as a religious subject than to the individual: we could say that God "thinks by groups." This is the theme of the covenant.

The covenant is called *"berit"* in Hebrew; it comes from an Assyrian word, *"birtu,"* which means "link." *Berit* is translated in Greek by *"syntheke,"* i.e., treaty, which corresponds to the Latin "*foedus*"; but it is also, and more frequently, translated by the Greek "*diatheke,*" i.e., testament (Latin "*testamentum*"), which corresponds to the English "last will and testament." The latter translation (*diatheke*) prevailed; it is the more accurate one, since it insists on God's initiative.

This covenant, as we have seen, was expressed through the metaphor of the Yahweh-Israel marriage. It was with Israel as a group that God contracted the covenant.

2. *Explanation of this dissonance.*

a) *The liberal school's explanation*: *a chronological development.*

The "liberal school" in exegesis flourished between 1850 and 1925 under the leadership of Wellhausen and B. Duhm. They insisted in particular on literary criticism, on the date of documents, and on the re-creation of the historical situation according to the principles of the theory of evolution.

In 1926, the appearance of Gunkel's commentary on the Psalms marked a turning point in criticism, which became "comparative," more "real," more mistrustful of purely literary criticism, as well as characterized by a very deep religious spirit. Today, on both the Protestant and Catholic sides, we are in a better position than fifty years ago.

For the liberal school, religious individualism did not exist in ancient Israel. Only from the time of Jeremiah and Ezekiel does the beginning of a relationship between the individual and his God appear.

A popularizer of this liberal explanation put it this way:

> The individual Israelite does not constitute the religious subject, but rather the whole people of Israel taken together. Only the misfortunes of the nation posed the question, ignored by the prophets, of how the lot of the individual is related, on the one hand, to his own actions, and, on the other, to the destiny of the whole people.

This explanation is untenable. We have already made it clear that the very existence of theophoric names is opposed to such a "chronological" explanation.

It will serve our purpose to begin with the first book of Samuel. The stage is set in the temple of Shiloh, and we see a sterile woman (who will be Samuel's mother) approaching to pray. Her prayer is supremely moving. We are conscious here of the individual manifesting herself in her piety:

> She was deeply distressed and prayed to the Lord, and wept bitterly. And she vowed a vow and said, "O Lord of hosts, if thou wilt indeed look on the affliction of thy maidservant, and remember me, and not forget thy maidservant, but wilt give to thy maidservant a son, then I will give him to the Lord all the days of his life, and no razor shall touch his head."

Now, as she was re-doubling her prayers before Yahweh, the priest Eli observed her mouth. Hannah spoke in her heart; only her lips were moving without uttering a word, and Eli thought that she was drunk. He said, "How long will you be drunken? Put away your wine from you." But Hannah replied, "No, my lord, I am a woman sorely troubled; I have drunk neither wine nor strong drink, but I have been pouring out my soul before the Lord. Do not regard your maidservant as a base woman, for all along I have been speaking out of my great anxiety and vexation." Eli replied, "Go in peace, and the God of Israel grant your petition which you have made to him" (I *Sm.* 1: 10-17).

The chronological explanation — as we see from this incident which took place well before the Exile — is, therefore, too rigid.

b) *A "dialectical" explanation must be adopted.*

The Hebrew mentality is so constituted that it likes to present in succession the variety of aspects of one single complex reality. In this process, obviously, thinking is not speculation or theorizing, but rather the translation of a real experience: it is a vital synthesis.

There is a succession of wavering from one aspect to another. Thus there arises a sort of "tension" within the process of reflection. Finally the mind reaches a state of equilibrium.

To give another example of this dialectical process: in the Bible there is a universalist outlook and a particularist outlook; they do not succeed one another according to a simple chronological scheme. Universalism exists side by side, throughout the whole Bible, with particularism. The "individual-community" tension must be understood in the same way.

II SURVEY OF THE HISTORY OF SALVATION — THREE PHASES IN THE OLD TESTAMENT

1. *Ancient Israel.*

During this first phase, emphasis is put upon the *idea of solidarity*: man is neither lost nor saved all alone.

Two reasons seem adequate to explain such great importance given to the idea of solidarity:

a) Among the Hebrews there were survivals of an *ancient solidarity.*

They had lived a life of nomadic collectivism, in which the individual was to the group what the limb is to the living body. A man does not live for himself nor by himself: the group is the true unity. In the desert the culpable act of an individual implicates his group, as well as its posterity. For example, the whole group is involved in seeking revenge.

The psychology and sociology of the Jews must be examined in the light of recent studies on "corporate personality." In the Bible, personages such as Adam, Abraham, and Jacob are presented as already sharing the experience of their descendants; their life is like a resumé of that of their posterity. For example, everything which we have seen of Adam — in our first three chapters — is applicable to all mankind as well.

Furthermore, we must take notice of the preference of the Semites for a more "existential" anthropology than ours, in which man is better understood in the context of his family and community relationships. See, for example, how Saul is described in I Samuel 9: 1-2: not only are his physical characteristics given, but also his community attachments (ancestors and tribe).

b) The *covenant*.

The explanations which have just been given, however, are not the most important. If, in the Bible, man appears immersed in a group, the reason is that the plan of Yahweh is presented as a *collective* plan: it is called the covenant.

The book of Deuteronomy gives the ideal explanation of the covenant and tries to place it in its original setting. Deuteronomy is a book which sprang from levitical reformers of the eighth century, an era when Israel was in the process of falling apart. These Levites, who represent the sacral tradition, wish to re-make Israel into a vast fraternity which will commemorate its glorious moments on the occasion of feasts. There will be no poor in those days: the orphan, the widow, the alien will all participate in the sacred banquets, and all will love one another.

War, in which man glories, is the occasion to show us, not a professional army, but a whole people under arms in Yahweh's name. In Deuteronomy the fault of one man harms the whole community. When the whole people is blamed, it is addressed as if it were a single person (cf. *Dt.* 29: 18).

In Deuteronomy the individual is seen behind the group; the group occupies first place. Each year the regular gathering of worshippers re-creates the atmosphere of Sinai, and re-enacts the answer of Israel to the call of its God: cf. Psalms 81 and 95, very similar in thought to Deuteronomy.

The prophets will repeat this, but they will do so in order to denounce sin. The prophets' point of view is more pessimistic; they present official reports of bankruptcy: the sins of generations long past, the sins of the desert, weigh upon the present. This is the picture of sin which the prophets paint, especially after Isaiah (read chapters 8 and 16 of Ezekiel). Sin becomes a hardening of the people (*Is.* 6: 9 ff.). Sin corrupts right down to the very roots of the people (*Jer.* 13). Sin is portrayed in that atrocious symphony of blood in Ezekiel 20: blood of murders, blood of injustices . . . .

All this accentuates the aspect of community and solidarity.

2. *From the Exile on.*

What is the meaning of the Exile (586-538)? It is a great moment of "retreat"; a great "favorable moment" (*kairos,* in Greek) when Yahweh will lift his people out of their sense of security, in order to be able to speak to them heart to heart.

The Exile brought together the most active elements of Israel: priests, prophets, middle class (metalworkers, carpenters), scribes, and officials. These several thousand people will eventually reach the point where they can — in response to the call of their prophets, especially of Jeremiah (already dead), Ezekiel, and the Second Isaiah (*Is.* 40-55) — reflect on the vocation of Israel. They will endeavor to become the "Remnant."

The expression "Remnant" indicates quality rather than number; there is nothing which prevents this Remnant from increasing and becoming a majority, but the expression is "qualitative." During the Exile the "qualitative Israel" begins to be formed.

The pattern we saw previously (the individual seen behind the group) will be reversed: Israel will be re-made, a qualitative Israel, beginning with individual "volunteers" (*nedabim*). The task of the prophets will be precisely to raise up these volunteers. We move now from the individual to the community — a community which is always called "Israel" (that old word which designates the people in its religious situation and which means "Let God show himself strong!").

Ezekiel, chapter 18, shows us that each individual must be morally sensitive and acknowledge his own responsibility. "I will judge you, O house of Israel, every one according to his ways" (18: 30). "House of Israel . . . every one": in the juxtaposition of these apparently contradictory terms we see an attempt to express both the personalism which will be stressed in the future and the sense of collectivity which is preserved from the past.

This is the same teaching which is found in the great proclamation of Jeremiah 31: 31-34, perhaps the greatest proclamation of the Old Testament, the most extraordinary promise. It is a promise of a new covenant, a covenant which will endure forever with Israel, but with an Israel which has been reconstituted on the basis of a "qualified" people.

> Behold, the days are coming, says the Lord, when I will make a new covenant with the house of Israel and the house of Judah, not like the covenant which I made with their fathers when I took them by the hand to bring them out of the land of Egypt, my covenant which they broke, though I was their husband, says the Lord. But this is the covenant which I will make with the house of Israel after those days, says the Lord: I will put my law within them, and I will write it upon their hearts; and I will be their God, and they shall be my people.

The most individualistic activity possible — God's dealing with each one's heart — will thus consist in the reconstitution of the covenant, with the same formula as the ancient covenant, "I will be their God and they shall be my people."

> And no longer shall each man teach his neighbor and each his brother, saying, "Know the Lord," for they shall all know me, from the least of them to the greatest, says the Lord; for I will forgive their iniquity.

There will be a "brand new" beginning, a work of grace, a "recharging of the spirit." And this will end with the establishment of a new Israel.

It is extremely interesting, from that point on, to observe what the disciples of these prophets of the new Israel (Jeremiah, Ezekiel, and the second Isaiah) did. Let us listen to them in the Psalter (they have exactly the same aim as the psalmist). For example, let us look at Psalm 149: "For the Lord takes pleasure in his people" (v. 4). "His people," i.e., the qualitative people, the "poor" (*anawim*) of sincere faith, the "just," the "pious" (*hasidim*).

It is a curious thing to discover that the most individualistic psalms, the ones in which the interior life of a soul shows forth most clearly, are also the psalms in which reference is made to the people of Israel: cf. Psalm 130 (our *De Profundis*), and Psalm 131 (the most beautiful psalm in the Bible), both of these psalms in which the psalmists, at the conclusion of the expression of their very personal piety, speak of Israel. The mystique of the covenant in its community aspect was never so tenacious as in this era of the greatest personal piety. The document most thoroughly penetrated with the spirit of the covenant comes to us from this epoch: chapter 16 of Leviticus, which contains a description of the feast of *Yom Kippur* (the great Day of Atonement), which received its final form only after the Exile. On this day each year there was an official return "to the state of the covenant," just as we make sure at Easter time that we are "in the state of grace."

3. *Judaism.*

a) The stage of Judaism is characterized by the presence and activity of the "sages." These are the men who took on the duty formerly exercised by the prophets: they are the guides of the people. They brought with themselves a heritage, the system of "distributive justice." The sages had been formed in an international and humanist tradition; their outlook did not include an immediate thought of "covenant," but rather was framed according to a religious system of distributive justice: I observe the law and I must be rewarded, I do not observe the law and I must be punished. This religion of the sages was not based on the history of salvation, which is proper to Israel, but rather upon the heritage common to the whole of the ancient Near East.

This point of view encountered the sacral vein of the religion of the covenant, which is based on history. The sages made the people of the covenant sensitive to a certain individualism, at the same time as they themselves turned toward the religion of the covenant (see below, chapter six).

This is, then, a new stone brought to the building which the prophets like Jeremiah and Ezekiel had begun to construct. The book of Daniel (165 B.C.), the "manifesto" of the sages, underscores the permanence of the community-individual tension: in this book Israel is "the people of the holy ones of the Most High" grouped around its martyrs.

b) This tension, this attempt at synthesis, this compromise can be recognized even in the eschatological outlook of the Jewish apocalypses (about fifty years after Christ). We see two stages of time:

First, the end of the world will bring the program of the covenant to fulfilment: Israel will finally arrive at its fullest development and make the Kingdom of God live here below; Israel will be reassembled about an extraordinary Jerusalem, which will appear on the occasion of the Messiah's coming and of his victory over the pagan nations. Israel will reign. For how long? Forty years . . . ? Four hundred years . . . ? After this the Messiah will die . . . . Israel has finished its task; it has blossomed into the Kingdom of God.

Then will begin the phase which involves all men, even those men to whom the Messiah was a complete stranger. For them the general judgment will take place, the judgment upon each of the works done by each individual in his own conscience; one just will go to Paradise and the wicked to Gehenna.

III THE NEW TESTAMENT

The New Testament does not reject any of these positions. Consequently, neither does it reject the tension between the individual and community. It raises both of them to their perfect expression. This will be easily seen in a study of three New Testament theologians, St. Paul, St. John, and the author of the Epistle to the Hebrews.

All three refer to the same text of Isaiah, chapter 53, which is perhaps the passage where the individual-community tension shows up the best. In this text we see an individual who takes upon himself the sins of the whole world; he comes out of Israel, and, in a certain sense, perhaps represents Israel. He is allied — yet alone. Thus, we see at one and the same time the victory of individualism and the victory of solidarity.

This is the text which Jesus relied on and the one in which he read his mission. And this text was taken up again by each of our three great "theologians."

The Epistle to the Hebrews applies to Christ the priest the passages which refer to the theology of expiation and especially the ritual of *Yom Kippur* (*Lv.* 16), to which Isaiah, chapter 53, had already referred.

St. Paul (*Rom.* 3: 25) wrote in reference to Christ Jesus the Redeemer:

> God put [him] forward as an expiation by his blood, to be received by faith. This was to show God's righteousness, because in his divine forbearance he had passed over former sins.

Once again the feast of Atonement is recalled, in which Christ is the bloody propitiation which brought the new covenant into being.

In St. John, Christ is the Lamb who bears the sins of the world. We have here again a reference to Isaiah, chapter 53 (cf. *Jn.* 1: 29).

It is interesting to note that all three authors make reference to this ritual of the feast of *Yom Kippur,* which put great stress on the community aspect. It is also interesting to note that, at the same time, the whole New Testament is presented as a commentary on that phrase of St. Paul, "He has loved me and has given himself up for me," which gives the strongest possible testimony to the individual aspect. The individual-community tension continues: it expresses our Christian life.

SUGGESTED READINGS

DeFraine, Jean, *Adam and the Family of Man,* Staten Island, New York: Alba House, 1965.

DeFraine, Jean, "Individu et société dans la religion de l'A. T." two articles in *Biblica,* 1952, pp. 324-355, 445-475.

Gelin, Albert, "Aspects communautaire et personnel du salut et du péché selon l'Ecriture" in *La Vie Commune,* Paris; Les Éditions du Cerf, 1952.

Gelin, Albert, *The Poor of Yahweh,* Collegeville, Minnesota: The Liturgical Press, 1964.

CHAPTER 5:

Man in the Covenant Situation: The Problem of Vocation

The very definition of the biblical man leads us to speak of the cooperation of man with God in the midst of the community; from a biblical parlance, this cooperation constitutes man's vocation.

I THE SCRIPTURAL FOUNDATION

1. *Israel's vocation.*

In laying a scriptural foundation of vocation, we must first show that Israel's vocation does exist.

Moses, in Exodus 19: 3-6, specified the nature of Israel's vocation:

> Thus you shall say to the house of Jacob, and tell the people of Israel: You have seen what I did to the Egyptians, and how I bore you on eagles' wings and brought you to myself. Now therefore, if you will obey my voice and keep my covenant, you shall be my own possession among all peoples; for all the earth is mine, and you shall be to me a kingdom of priests and a holy nation. These are the words which you shall speak to the children of Israel.

This is Israel's program, this is Israel's vocation: to be a *witness-people* of God; the people through which he will realize his revolutionary plan of communicating with humanity, of entering into dialogue with it — in a word, the covenant. The Old Testament and the New Testament: this is the covenant.

"You will be my witness-people." And, as a result, you will be my *"filter-people."* You will filter out of humanity everything that is good in its intellectual endeavor and in its institutions: a filtering of myths and of religious strivings, a filtering, too, of magic and of divination, a filtering of sacrificial customs. Yes, this will be a people which assimilates, but to guide this process of assimilation there will be a criterion which is a part of their lives; this criterion is the covenant.

Witness-people, filter-people, and, as will be affirmed at a later date, *missionary-people* as well: this is Israel's vocation.

We can define Israel in St. Paul's words (I *Cor.* 3: 9): "We are fellow workers for God," who have been invited to take part actively in the love of God, in his plan of love. This is what Israel is. The prophets convey this idea very well when they speak of the marriage of Yahweh and Israel. This marriage is not merely an attractive and sentimental image which has an emotional "aura" clinging to it; rather, it clearly indicates the concept of a shared task, which is to reach its fulfilment in the Kingdom of God. Israel is the builder of the Kingdom of God (along with God, of course); it is for this that Israel was chosen.

We see that this vocation becomes more profound and better understood through the whole length of Israel's history. In this connection I must bring to your attention that great "recapitulation," that great meditation on the vocation of Israel which is found in chapters 40 to 55 of Isaiah. (For the "terminology of vocation" see especially Isaiah 41: 9; 42: 6; 48: 12; 50: 2; 51: 2.) A meditation on certain events, the Abraham event, the Moses event, the David event, the Jeremiah event: these are the four landmarks.

Just as, for example, on the night before a religious profession or ordination, we think over the events which have happened in our past (those events which are for us signs and traces of God in our lives, which have become clear as we look back on them), so it was for Israel: the events known as the call of Abraham, the exodus from Egypt, the triumph of David, the suffering of Jeremiah, all take on grandeur and stand out more conspicuously once Israel looks back on them in its past. But they did not seem so clear to Israel at the actual moment when it lived them!

It is thus that Israel, guided during the Exile by its prophet, the Second Isaiah (chapters 40-55), was led by these events of the past to devote itself to a meditation on its vocation. The past becomes a call of God in the present, an authoritative demand of God on his witness-people, his filter-people, his missionary-people. Israel itself enters more deeply into the possession of its vocation and sees it more clearly. This is because the development of a vocation requires external stimuli. And one of the most important of these was the Exile: Israel reduced to zero by the Exile, Israel discovering the world and consequently discovering missionary opportunity. All of this is a gift of the Lord, like a providential circumstance, a *kairos*.

I would say that the vocation of the Church is no way different, for the Church is, as St. Paul says, "the Israel of God"; to her the covenant is confided, with all that this implied and more, and all this to a degree of profundity never before realized. The Church has the responsibility of the dialogue which God wishes to carry on with man through her. The Church must succeed!

2. *Vocation of the "great men" of Israel.*

Such are the broad lines of the canvas upon which we are going to "pin" or "embroider" the outlines of certain special, concrete vocations, those of the "great men" who came forth from Israel.[1]

---

1. Cf. A. Gelin, *Hommes et Femmes de la Bible,* Paris; Editions Ligel, "Horizons de la catéchèse" collection. In this important volume will be found the further development of what is touched upon here. *Original editor's note.*

I will mention only the best known vocations:

The vocations of Abraham and Moses. Their calls must be put together because they are the saints who are familiar to all. Every essential element is found in their vocations: a call — a life directed to a single goal — a striving for the common good, for the covenant. All these are elements which I am going to analyze.

Next comes the select group of the great prophets: Isaiah, Jeremiah, Ezekiel. It is easy to see in their case what vocation is: a reality that moves forward, that progressively grows. A vocation is not a book in our pocket, printed once and for all for everybody; it is not a static element, but rather a life that is moving along, the direction and the thrust of a life, a life brought together into unity before God.

There is, finally, a privileged group of vocations in the era of the New Testament, vocations of those who, each in his turn, have advanced the plan of God: Mary, Peter, Paul . . . .

I have tried to choose the more outstanding vocations, but we must not minimize the others:

No vocation is more sharply defined than that of Amos; every essential element is found (cf. *Am.* 7: 14-15). Amos responds to the priest Amaziah, who is casting him out of the sanctuary of Bethel: "I am no prophet, nor a prophet's son; but I am a herdsman, and a dresser of sycamore trees, and the Lord took me from following the flock, and the Lord said to me, 'Go, prophesy to my people Israel.' "

Then, there is also Jonah! If there is any book which makes us understand what God's call is, it is the book of Jonah. This is the model of the missionary vocation. Jonah is a type, a symbol of the man who has received the call and who must answer it whether he wants to or not.

These scriptural notions, which we shall take up in greater detail, are fundamental ones, but they are also ones which lead on to further development: the vocation of Israel to assist God's plan, and, on the other hand, built upon this foundation, the vocation of those who were personally called in Israel to serve this plan of God. From these notions I shall draw a "theology of vocation."

II FROM THESE SCRIPTURAL NOTIONS: A THEOLOGY OF VOCATION

What is vocation in the biblical sense?

1. *Vocation: God's gift and God's initiative.*

a) It is a call, an election .... All this is, as it were, "incrusted" in the word "vocation." It is a gift (an act of love). We offer a few examples to illustrate this:

Let us take Jeremiah 1: 5, "Before I formed you in the womb I knew you." "Knew": this term corresponds to Israel's vocation. Compare Amos 3: 2, "You only have I known of all the families of the earth; therefore I will punish you for all your iniquities." (= I have cherished you with my love, you the Israelites, and that is why, just as — in the Israelite world — a husband punishes his wife, I punish you for your sins.) But here, in Jeremiah, the "knowing" of Yahweh has become very personal; there is a penetration into the secret life of Jeremiah: initiative of God, love, goodness of God — all this is suggested by the word "know."

Let us go on: "Before you were born I consecrated you." "Consecrated": there is no question here of sanctifying grace being infused into Jeremiah. Nor is there any question of the removal of original sin (there was no awareness at all of original sin at that time). No! "Consecrated" means "set apart for a religious task." What task? "I appointed you a prophet to the nations."

We see, through Jeremiah's example, how far the call of grace goes (this election is portrayed here with an uncommon profusion of details). It is truly an initiative of God, a freely given grace, a creation of God, who seems to take no account of human worth. To make us understand this choice of God, St. Paul, who is such a theorist, will tell us:

> Consider your call, brethren . . . . God chose what is foolish in the world to shame the wise, God chose what is weak in the world to shame the strong, God chose what is low and despised in the world, even things that are not, to bring to nothing things that are, so that no human being might boast in the presence of God.
>
> (I *Cor.* 1: 26-29)

"God has chosen!"

b) Generally speaking, this call is adapted to an individual's psychological framework and makes allowances for it. God calls each man according to his personal qualifications. It is from this point of view that we should study, in St. John's psychologically perceptive first chapter, the call of the first apostles:

The call of John, that delicate adolescent, who turns to Jesus and does not dare to say, "Who are you?" but says to him, "Rabbi, where are you staying?" It is four o'clock in the afternoon; he goes and stays with Jesus. His whole psychological outlook is already involved in his call; there, close to Jesus, he began to show what will be his distinctive characteristic as an apostle, "staying with him."

There is Kephas, Peter, who craves activity. The Lord sees that right away. He fixes a telling glance on Peter and says, "You are Simon! You will be called Peter," that is, the one suited for use as a foundation. This is the call of the man of action.

There is also the call of the intellectual, Nathanael, whose ironic comment was perhaps a cover-up for tenderness or for concern. Jesus calls him in his turn: you will see greater things than these, you will see divine secrets, you will see the heavens in league with the earth (= you will understand the covenant, you will understand the Incarnation, you will understand Christianity). How well this call is adapted to a particular temperament!

c) I said, "this call"; I should have said, "these calls." For the call is repeated. We could read the history of Israel as the history of a call continually repeated — with God, on his part, never becoming weary: "I extended my hands to you all the day long but you were unwilling."

But let us read together, in rapid fashion, as a parable, the repeated calls made to St. Peter. The one we just read was the quasi-secret call; the official call takes place by the Sea of Galilee near Capernaum: "You will be fishers of men" (*Mt.* 4: 19). The most moving call, when everyone had abandoned Jesus after the setback in Galilee: 'Who do you say that I am? . . . You are the Christ, the Son of the living God' (*Mt.* 16: 15-16). The call which was only a glance, in the house of the high priest (*Lk.* 22: 61). The call, finally, to his love, a love deeper than the weakness of the 'flesh,' the call which makes him 'shepherd of his lambs and his sheep' (*Jn.* 21: 15-17).

2. *Vocation*: *the unifying factor in life.*

a) A prophet's vocation is often announced in his "inaugural vision," which already contains in germ what the life of the prophet will realize in dramatic fashion. This is very obvious in the case of Isaiah (chapter 6). He will be the preacher of the holy, transcendent God; the preacher of the "Remnant," of the qualified "little Remnant"; the proclaimer as well of the hardening of Israel's heart, to which he will give a "classic" expression (*Is.* 6: 9-10). All this is already contained in his inaugural vision, which is, as it were, a condensed version of his future preaching. We know neither where nor in what circumstances this inaugural vision was put into written form, but it was most likely five or six years after the event, about 734 B.C. But all his preaching is already there in germ.

Consider how St. Paul spoke of his own call in his Epistle to the Galatians (1: 15-16). It is short but contains all the essential elements, even some seventeen years after the event. The life of St. Paul was a confirmation of that call. "But when he who had set me apart before I was born, and had called me through his grace, was pleased to reveal his Son in me, in order that I might preach him among the Gentiles. . . ." The two essential characteristics of Pauline preaching are present there in germ, viz., the missionary role among the pagans, and the doctrine of Christ within Paul and within the Christian, of Christ not only the harvest, but also the sap.

b) A second characteristic note is that, after this inaugural vision, the life of the one who has been called, the life of his vocation, is a life of discovery in the faith. In the faith! The Virgin Mary, who "lived in faith as we" (as Theresa of the Child Jesus expressed it) and who was not a goddess, verifies this spiritual law.

Perhaps most interesting of all in the Old Testament, from this point of view, is the life of Jeremiah. Why? Because he is one of the rare Semites who, with Nehemiah (but Nehemiah to a lesser degree) makes us enter into his interior life, who has told us the story of this life in his "Confessions," which, except for its length, reminds us of the "Confessions" of St. Augustine. It occupies about four chapters, in which we hear Jeremiah speaking to himself, or, rather, in dialogue with God, always with trust, but sometimes in an extremely harsh tone, such as is used by very intimate friends of God. "O Lord, thou hast deceived me, and I was deceived; thou art stronger than I, and thou hast prevailed" (*Jer.* 20: 7). Deception and conflict: that is Jeremiah's life. Then, one day, we see him completely discouraged; it is hard to participate in God's love, to be a supporter of the covenant, to be a "collaborator of God," as St. Paul will say. He had the whole world on his shoulders: the generals, the leaders, who called him defeatist, the priests, who called him "impious," the prophets, too, whom he must contradict, the officials, and especially the king — none of these will help. He had no friends, no wife to strengthen him. His prophetic task is to proclaim the "visit" of Yahweh. He is repulsed and ignored, the kids rag him in the streets of Jerusalem. Ah! he can endure no longer!

> Woe is me, my mother, that you bore me, a man of strife and contention to the whole land! . . . all of them curse me . . . .
> O Lord, thou knowest;
> remember me and visit me,
> and take vengeance for me on my persecutors.
> In thy forbearance take me not away;
> know that for thy sake I bear reproach.
> Thy words were found, and I ate them,
> and thy words became to me a joy
> and the delight of my heart;
> for I am called by thy name,
> O Lord, God of hosts.
> I did not sit in the company of merrymakers,
> nor did I rejoice;
> I sat alone, because thy hand was upon me,
> for thou hadst filled me with indignation.
> Why is my pain unceasing,
> my wound incurable,
> refusing to be healed?
> Wilt thou be to me like a deceitful brook,
> like waters that fail?

Then Yahweh answered him:

> If you return, I will restore you,
> and you shall stand before me.
> If you utter what is precious, and not what is worthless,
> you shall be as my mouth.
> They shall turn to you,
> but you shall not turn to them.
> And I will make you to this people
> a fortified wall of bronze;
> they will fight against you,

but they shall not prevail over you.
for I am with you
to save you and deliver you.

(*Jer.* 15: 10-20)

It is striking that this text takes up the same words as the inaugural vision (*Jer.* 1: 8, 18-19). Does God ever say two different things? No! it is always the same thing which he takes up again and repeats. We could say that, once he has relied upon someone, he never repents of this; he begins again to rely, and he demands of his elect that he be "converted." Such is the vocation of Jeremiah, a hard vocation, which is interwoven with suffering and is a painful discovery in faith.

Let us take up the example of Mary. What is Mary's life, after the Magnificat and the Visitation, except an onward march? The Magnificat of her seventeen years, the Magnificat which St. Augustine declares was composed by our "tambourine-player" (*tympanistria nostra*), like her ancestor Miriam after Yahweh's great deed (*Ex.* 15). The Magnificat which was the commentary on her inaugural vision, that vision which informed her of the exact role which the Lord wanted her to play: to be the mother of the Messiah and the mother of the people of the Messiah. As a matter of fact, when the angel had spoken of this messianic motherhood, he referred to the old texts of Isaiah (cf. *Lk.* 1: 31-32 and *Is.* 7: 14; 9: 5-6). Isaiah 7:14 treats of the mother of the king (Messiah), the *gebira,* the *"grande dame,"* she who has a special standing, she who gathers the people around the king, her son. The Virgin Mary saw this, obscurely but really, for the Magnificat is above all a commentary on this second, or community aspect, of her vocation. The Magnificat speaks almost exclusively of the People of God, that people of believers composed of the heirs of Abraham, composed of the "poor," of those who are open to God, free from that prideful rigidity which is the product of riches and the exercise of power.

Mary knew all this, but she knew it as a young girl of seventeen; she had to grow in understanding of it all her life. It is precisely in this that the Gospels of Luke and of John are harmonious and complementary; we see how, little by little, she attributes greater importance to this second aspect of her vocation, just as more and more until the Cross (*Jn.* 19: 25-27) she discovers what it is to be the mother of the People of God, their spiritual mother . . . . For suffering plays a very great role in the discovery of vocation ("He learned obedience through what he suffered," was said of Christ, in Hebrews 5: 8).

Vocation is, therefore, the unifying factor in one's life; and I would say that, if it is the unifying factor of a life, it is the happiness of a life, since happiness is caused by success in life.

3. *Vocation: always (in the Bible) a function of the common good.*

a) It is given for the community, then inserted as a "function" into the development of the covenant; it is a contract and, therefore, a service, a duty.

Should I explain this truth better and at greater length than I have already done? There is only one thing which counts, in Israel; it is the covenant, the dialogue with God, that dialogue which, one day, will be made easier, since God himself will come to take his place on both sides of the dialogue. What I mean is this: Christ Jesus, the God-Man, has come, the only one able to take part in the dialogue and make it succeed. That is why vocation is always at the service of the covenant, of the covenant more or less fulfilled, fulfilled marvelously with the coming of Christ Jesus, but, "in this curious case" (in Peguy's words), finding itself in need of our efforts. God has need of men!

I think that it is necessary to comment on this assertion in a very concrete, i.e., typically biblical, fashion, by reference to the life of Jeremiah, to the great parable of Jonah, or more simply to the Second Epistle to the Corinthians, in which Paul's example shows us what it is to make an all-out effort when one has been bitten by the love of God and wishes to share in his work.

b) Special duties, "specialized vocation." The goal is the common good; the means, specialized tasks: this is the message of the New Testament. In I Corinthians 12, notice how St. Paul enumerates these vocations, with his relish for classification (what a consolation for me! for I, too, love to classify and distinguish!). "There is one and the same Spirit," without doubt, but see what different tasks there are, all at the service of the welfare of the whole Mystical Body (cf. also *Rom.* 12).

But, before Paul, the Old Testament had also shown us "specialized vocations." The sphere of work is sometimes very restricted; the task assigned is a very precise task:

recall Jonah, for example, who was commissioned to attacking paganism in its presumed center, that counterpart of Babel that was Nineveh;

recall, on the other hand, those who were restricted to Israel, to one or another particular area, e.g., Amos, who was required to work only in the Northern Kingdom.

III CONCLUSION: THE "VOCATION" OF JESUS

Perhaps we should conclude with a consideration of the vocation of Jesus (*Lk.* 4: 17-20), Jesus "sent," Jesus with his simple life, his life without fault, his life without failures, silences, with that seeming total failure, the Cross.

If you wish to study this vocation of Jesus, which we look upon as the ideal vocation, vocation reaching its highest degree of concentration, if you wish to have an idea of this vocation of Jesus, place yourself at a particularly important moment, that of his final farewell (*Jn.* 13: 1).

Tomorrow will be the Passion, tomorrow he will rise towards his Father, tomorrow he will be "lifted up." At that moment, there is an unprecedented richness of concentration: the whole past of his people comes to life again before him. What past? The Passover: "Knowing that his hour was come, that he should pass out of this world to the Father" (*Jn.* 13: 1). "Pass"? Did Israel ever do anything but pass? Pass from Egypt to Canaan, pass from Canaanite life to Israelite life, pass from the Exile to the Holy Land. The Passover, the Pasch is at the center of his thought, that Pasch which he celebrated with his own in a very human fashion.

The covenant is also at the center of his thought: "This is my blood, the blood of the new covenant"! Jesus' vocation is situated within Israel's vocation, within its unique task: the covenant! Or, better, Jesus' vocation fully absorbs Israel's vocation: Israel was made for Jesus.... And when Jesus says, "This is the covenant in my blood, my blood shed for you," what image did he have in his thoughts? The image of *Yom Kippur,* the image of Atonement, the image of that return to the "state of the covenant," every year during the fall. This annual renewal expresses in symbol all the sacrifices which lead to the Cross. This, then, is Jesus' vocation: to absorb Israel's vocation, to bring it to a conclusion.

What then? John tells us (13: 1) that Jesus "loved his own who were in the world...." Did God himself — God, a being of tenderness, the tenderness of a mother (*rahamin*) —do otherwise in the Old Testament? Christ shares in this love of God, he is defined as God, he carries within himself that love of God, or, even better, he *is* the love of God made flesh. This is his vocation, which is linked with the past, linked with Israel's vocation. After all, this is perhaps what vocation is: the following of a direction already set, a liaison with all the labor already performed, but also a new aspect, and perhaps the adding of the last note.

SUGGESTED READINGS

DeFraine, Jean, *The Bible on Vocation and Election,* De Pere, Wisc.: St. Norbert Abbey Press, 1966.

Gelin, Albert, "La vocation, étude biblique" in *Ami du clergé,* 1959, pp. 161-164.

Jeanne d'Arc, Soeur, "Le mystère de la vocation" in *Vie Spirituelle,* Feb. 1965, pp. 167-186.

Poelman, R., *Esquisse biblique du mystère de la vocation* (cahiers de la Roseraie), Brussels, 1956. pp. 9-52.

Powis Smith, J. M., "The Chosen People" in *American Journal of Semitic Languages and Literature* 45, 1928-29, 73 ff.

Rowley, H. H., *The Biblical Doctrine of Election,* London, 1950.

Stendahl, Krister, "The Called and the Chosen: An Essay on Election" in *The Root of the Vine* (essays in biblical theology), by Anton Fridrichsen et al. New York: Philosophical Library, 1953.

CHAPTER 6:

The Problem of Faith: The Three Attitudes of the Sages

This chapter will bear upon the problem of faith, since the biblical man is defined by faith.

I THE BIBLICAL MAN IS DEFINED BY FAITH

Faith is an "upward gesture." The Bible accustoms us to this "upward gesture," even in the situations of affliction in which we so often see biblical personages.

1. *The two "aspects" of faith.*

Faith appears in the Bible under two aspects: the supporting aspect and the dynamic aspect.

a) The *supporting aspect* is translated by the Hebrew root *emet*. The word *"veritas"* (truth), which appears so often in the liturgy, is not a very good translation of *emet*. *Emet* means "solidity": I lean upon God as upon a solid reality, not as upon a rotten staff. I have faith, I am called one of the faithful (*emun*), one who *leans upon* .... The word *"Amen"* from the same root means: it is firm! and consequently, it is true!

b) The *dynamic aspect* is especially emphasized in the Psalter. A hundred times we find the word "*batah,*" which means "to have trust," "to rely on." A word much more dynamic than *emet*, which rather evokes the notion of rest, *batah* corresponds to *fiducia* in Latin (trust, reliance). Let us take the example of Psalm 131. It treats of a "poor man," who, having arrived at the end of his life, does evil no longer and commits himself to God "like a child quieted on its mother's breast." You have noticed the dynamic "aliveness" of someone who is not blasé: a baby on its mother's lap is certainly not blasé! *Batah!*

This is faith in the Bible: support and dynamism.

2. *Faith is directed to the God of the covenant.*

Faith is directed not to the God of the philosophers, but to the God of Abraham and Isaac and Jacob, that God who is tender, that God who involves himself in the future of man, that God who is interested in us, who acts as a broker for mankind, the God of exploits, who is "right in there"!

In this connection, it is interesting to consider a very old text inserted into Deuteronomy (you perhaps know that the books of the Bible often contain old material, and, in all likelihood, we have here one of the oldest sections of the Bible). It treats of the prayer which the Israelite says as he brings forward his basket of first fruits, not at the sanctuary of Jerusalem, but in the sanctuaries of the countryside where a Levite collects the gifts. It is very striking to see how this Creed is presented (for that is what it is). The Creed is an act of faith in Yahweh's deeds: Yahweh who acted in the past, Yahweh who is acting now, Yahweh who will act in time to come. You must, moreover, read the whole passage in its context, which we shall not quote here. You will find there, repeated eleven times, the expression, "Yahweh your God"; it is not another God, not Baal — not just any god — but Yahweh your God, who gives you the first fruits of the earth. We perceive with admiration, in this text, the action of the Levites, who were the ones who wove the Yahwist tapestry in Israel. But let us listen to the ancient Creed:

> And you shall go to the priest who is in office at that time,

> and say to him, " I declare this day to the Lord your God that I have come into the land which the Lord swore to our fathers to give us." Then the priest shall take the basket from your hand, and set it down before the altar of the Lord your God.
>
> And you shall make response before the Lord your God, "A wandering Aramean was my father; and he went down into Egypt and sojourned there, few in number; and there he became a nation, great, mighty, and populous. And the Egyptians treated us harshly, and afflicted us, and laid upon us hard bondage. Then we cried to the Lord the God of our fathers, and the Lord heard our voice, and saw our affliction, our toil, and our oppression; and the Lord brought us out of Egypt with a mighty hand and an outstretched arm, with great terror, with signs and wonders; and he brought us into this place and gave us this land, a land flowing with milk and honey. And behold, now I bring the first fruit of the ground, which thou, O Lord, hast given me.
>
> (*Dt.* 26: 3-10)

This is the Israelite Creed. This Creed is addressed precisely to that God who brought about Israel's series of exploits which accomplished the "redemption," i.e., the departure from Egypt. Let us not forget this absolutely essential fact, that the Exodus is at the center of Israel's piety (see also Psalms 81 and 85).

3. *The God to whom we turn can be reached through signs.*

God the Savior is in contact with us today by means of signs. These "signs of faith" are not lacking. We are surrounded by them until the moment which Psalm 74, composed during the Exile, recalls sadly: "We do not see our signs" (*Ps.* 74: 9).

What, then, are God's permanent signs?

The *Temple,* in which every year the history of the covenant is relived; the Temple, which is like the center of the earth (*Ez.* 38) where Yahweh made his name dwell (*Jer.* 7).

The theocratic *Royalty,* which was chosen by the prophets, then by Yahweh (*Ps.* 2: 6).

History, which leads us to him and which is his "sacrament."

The *Torah,* living word of God.

The *seasons* in their stability; ever since Yahweh stopped the action of his "bow" (the rainbow) and laid down his "arrow machine" (lightning), men have been reunited with God (*Gn.* 8: 22; *Acts.* 14: 17). More broadly, it is the *"sign of creation"* which makes this dialogue possible (*Acts.* 17: 26; *Rom.* 1: 20).

These signs are permanent. There are others, of course, which manifest the Lord to us, signs which, sometimes, cannot be expressed in words and which are often clear only to those who receive them. The Old Testament refers to these with the term *"ot,"* a sign. This type of sign, which appears in an infinite variety of forms, initiates an encounter, as, for example, when Samuel gave a sign to Saul in the name of God (I *Sm.* 9, 10). The sign for Elijah will be a light breeze, thanks to which an attentive soul is reunited with God. The sign, says Job, is the wheat which God causes to spring up. The sign is the swaddling clothes of a Child, which the angels gave to the shepherds of Bethlehem to bring about an encounter with God. Everything in the Old Testament and the New Testament is an occasion for an "upward gesture."

4. *The "heroes" of faith.*

a) Abraham — throughout the Bible, he is the "father of believers." Abraham always believed in God, even in the most unexpected, the most unforeseen situations (the most absurd situations, says Kierkegaard in his book *Fear and Trembling*). "Abraham believed God, and it was reckoned to him as righteousness" (*Rom.* 4: 3). You know that famous text (*Gn.* 15: 6) which St. Paul used to tie all Christianity, in its very foundations, to Abraham.

Abraham's adventure as a believer has been well summed up in the Epistle to the Hebrews, chapter 11. Abraham is rather peacefully settled; he lives off in the East, the civilized East. He is not at the very center of civilized life but is on the outskirts of the cities, in the immediate vicinity of Ur or of Haran. And, behold, the Lord says to him, "Come, leave your home! Become a wanderer, set out haphazardly!" Abraham *believed*. While he was leading that life of adventure, in the "land of your sojournings," as the P document has it, i.e., the land where one does not have his own habitation, Yahweh promised him an heir, since he must become the father of a great nation. This, too, is attributed to his faith: "Shall a child be born to a man who is a hundred years old? Shall Sarah, who is ninety years old, bear a child?" (*Gn.* 17: 17). They both laughed, Sarah especially. This laugh of Abraham has made the rabbis very uncomfortable: it is a laugh of satisfaction, not of unbelief, they said . . . . So Abraham did believe, and he had a son, an heir.

An unforeseen situation: to run the risks of a father of a family at that age! (I am taking the text just as it is, not subjecting it to critical analysis at this time.) But this heir must be sacrificed (a still more unforeseen situation). This is a divine command, an inspiration which comes to him, as a religious pressure in this land where the first born are sacrificed. He submits, believing against all hope; and his son is given back to him.

Such is Abraham's faith: we understand, afterwards, that his had been a "typical" faith. We continue to look at it, to contemplate it. Genesis 15: 6 was not written in Abraham's time, but in the Yahwist era, about the tenth century before Christ.

b) Isaiah — I have chosen Isaiah, since his faith follows the same pattern as Abraham's. The faith in question here is not a personal affair (in the sense that the hero of faith will be concerned for his personal destiny); the concern here is for the destiny of the people. Their faith is hinged on this: Abraham is a "father," Isaiah is a prophet, a commentator on the passing scene, we might almost say one who "triggers" the event. Isaiah is "the prophet of faith," as Abraham is "the father of believers." The slogan of Isaiah: Here it is: "If you will not believe, you shall not endure" (*Is.* 7: 9b). *Without belief, no existence!* Faith, for him, consists in uprooting all the supports which made the life of the nation comfortable and in turning towards what he calls "the waters of Shiloah that flow gently" (*Is.* 8: 6), those waters of Shiloah, symbol of Yahweh. Faith is a turning towards the Temple (very unpretentious at that), where a "rock" is found, covered with instructions for the believers.

Therefore hear the word of the Lord, you scoffers,
who rule this people in Jerusalem!
Because you have said, "We have made a covenant with death,
and with Sheol we have an agreement;
when the overwhelming scourge passes through
it will not come to us;
for we have made lies our refuge,
and in falsehood we have taken shelter";
therefore thus says the Lord God,
"Behold, I am laying in Zion for a foundation
a stone, a tested stone,
a precious cornerstone, of a sure foundation.
(*Is.* 28: 14-16)

Now, what is written on this rock, or, rather, what is the rock's name? It is this: "He who believes will not be in haste" (*Is.* 28: 16). Everywhere we look in Isaiah we find this "slogan of faith."

To have faith is very fine! But will we see Isaiah in such critical situations as Abraham? Yes, he does find himself in such situations. These are the sadest days in Israel's history, before the great siege of 587; we are now in 701: Judah had shrunk like a piece of leather; the Assyrian armies were besieging Jerusalem, which was at the point of imminent surrender. The emissaries of the Assyrian king came to the base of the ramparts, jeering at the people who had been reduced, as they said, to eating their excrement and drinking "the water of their feet" (their urine). At this moment Isaiah's faith rises to a high pitch:

> Therefore thus says the Lord concerning the king of Assyria: He shall not come into this city . . . . For I will defend this city to save it, for my own sake, and for the sake of my servant David.
>
> (*Is.* 37: 33-35)

That moment is a great one when, very unexpectedly, faith makes its "upward gesture."

5. *Faith of the man at grips with his own destiny.*

I have taken as models of faith, Abraham and Isaiah, who were national heroes, fathers of their people. Now I will consider the faith of man face to face with his own destiny.

a) Let us consider Job first. It is not at all important to know whether Job is a historical figure or not, or to ask ourselves whether there was, on the borders of Edom, a rich Bedouin named Job. The personage Job, as he is depicted in the book of Job, is above all a literary type, one of the "Poor of Yahweh"; it is in this light that he has meaning.

The Job of the biblical poem lost his possessions and his family, one after the other. His wife alone was left to him; and, as often in the Bible, she is there to stir him up rather than to soothe him. His health has been taken away; he has contracted a kind of elephantiasis. He has lost his reputation . . . he has lost his "theology," too, i.e., that final support which allows us to understand something that happens to us. He has lost his theology, that imperfect theology of that age which linked together sin and suffering, virtue and happiness. No, says Job, I do not understand at all! He has lost his last support; he is in an utterly absurd situation, in an unforeseen situation with no way out.

What then? He finds his faith again, pure faith, which is adherence to God, to God himself, to God caught sight of without signs, without consolations, without God's rewards: *Ipsissimus Deus!* God, himself, nothing but him. He has saved religion, he has saved faith. Chapter 42 shows him exhausted at last, in silence. "I have talked too much, I uttered folly! and now I am silent!"

> Therefore I have uttered what I did not understand,
> things too wonderful for me, which I did not know . . . .
> therefore I despise myself,
> and repent in dust and ashes.
>
> (*Jb.* 42: 3, 6)

b) That faith of Job is exactly the same as the faith of the "Poor of Yahweh." Read for example Psalm 88; you will see that faith, the faith of a "poor fellow" who can endure no longer, who has no more hope, who "blasphemes." But if he had no more faith at all, he would be silent. No! he must cry out. If he cries, he wishes to be heard. The "blood of Abel" expresses itself, it cries out! Read also Psalms 131 and 73 . . . and look upon that cortege, all that endless company.[1]

II THE JOURNEY OF THE SAGES OF ISRAEL

I attach great importance to this second part of this chapter, which will help us penetrate into the secret of Israel's faith through a kind of counterproof: [2] we are going to examine the rather curious behavior of the sages of Israel, who become more and more perfectly converted to the faith of the covenant. Let us try to retrace this curious journey in three stages.

1. *First stage*: *the sages before the Exile.*

The sages (*hakamim*) are those who excel in "counsel" (*esah*)

---

1. See Albert Gelin, *The Poor of Yahweh* (Collegeville, Minn.: The Liturgical Press, 1964).

2. In engraving, a counterproof is a reversed print taken from an ordinary fresh proof by contact impression and used to study the state of the engraved plate. *Trans.*

(*Jer.* 18: 18), i.e., in the use of their reason. They set up schools. To understand them we must evoke their native environment, that "university" atmosphere which is attested to, from the year 3000, in Egypt as well as Sumer; in this latter land, there were lay "universities" in addition to the "universities" connected with temples.

a) Instruction was given there principally on how to pursue a career in government. In Egypt all the officials of the state went through these schools. They became superintendents, foremen of work gangs, tax collectors, couriers, ambassadors. Many languages were taught, and it was understood that only those who graduated from these schools were assigned to the field of international relations.

b) With regard to human problems, there was a humanist morality which they studied deeply and handed down. You must realize that morality is not a biblical monopoly, and that the Decalogue itself is linked with an international morality, a human morality. I recognize, of course, that the Decalogue is something else besides; it is the law of a nation which is in the process of gestation, which needs to have its own rhythm, its own sacred laws, but, even so, there is in the Decalogue itself the perpetuation of an international morality.

c) The instruction was basically religious. They talked of "divinity," and sometimes this even took on a monotheistic tone: *the* god, they said . . . .

d) Obviously they knew how to write; they became "scribes" (*sopherim*). When they had studied in Canaan, they learned to write very rapidly. A Canaanite scribe (consequently pre-Israelite) was called "a nimble scribe," a rapid writer. This was such a commendation that the Egyptians took this term directly into their language, transcribing it just as it was, without translating it. The "nimble scribe" was an export commodity. In the time of the Canaanites, before the coming of Israel (the country was even more civilized than in the time of Israel), there was a city called Qiryat-Sepher, "City of the Book" (qiryat = city, cf. Carthage, "the new city"), or, perhaps, "City of the Scribe" (*Jos.* 15: 15).

The developing royalty of Israel will seek its officials from among the sages. The sages were the builders of the Israelite state. There was a scribe of Babylonian origin at David's court. Dismiss any idea that there was in David's time any sort of racism in Israel; there was, instead, a mixture of peoples (the "Jewish race" is Hitler's invention). To be sure, at a particular time after the Exile a religiously-based racism was experienced, but not in David's time. The Israelite royalty apparently molded itself after the Egyptian administrative pattern.

The scribes are "religious," without doubt, but, as we have pointed out above, they do not take their deepest inspiration from the sacral tradition: they are Yahwists "in the rough," if I may so express it. Yes or no, are we going to found a state? If we found it, we must have an army that can do the job: David will go to seek the nucleus of his army among the Philistines. And then, we must establish fortresses, build a fleet, get ready for war, enter into alliances, and the king must have many wives to have many children who will be married off in courts near and far. There you have politics! The sages are politicians, men of astuteness. "Wisdom," in the time of David and Solomon, could often be translated by "competency," "political competency," or even "political know-how." To be wise means to be a shrewd man and not necessarily a moral one.

You understand that tension could not but be generated; there is going to be a battle between the sacral tradition and the international and humanist tradition of the sages. This wisdom is a "foreign body" to be "digested." Who will be the digester"?

While waiting for the answer to this question, let us see a bit of the style of the battle. Let us listen above all to Isaiah, then to Jeremiah.

Isaiah cannot stand the sages. The word "wisdom," which can be found in any concordance, is particularly rich in pejorative meanings. When Isaiah speaks of Egypt, the fatherland of the sages, of the bureaucrats, he cuts them to pieces:

The princes of Zoan are utterly foolish;
  the wise counselors of Pharaoh give stupid counsel.
How can you say to Pharaoh, "I am a son of the wise,
  a son of ancient kings?"
Where then are your wise men?
  Let them tell you and make known
  what the Lord of hosts has purposed against Egypt.
The princes of Zoan have become fools,
  and the princes of Memphis are deluded;
those who are the cornerstones of her tribes
  have led Egypt astray.
The Lord has mingled within her a spirit of confusion.
(*Is.* 19: 11-14)

This is a criticism not only of sages who lived far away but also of those whom he had right before his eyes. For there is a struggle between Isaiah, who wanted to be the "gray eminence" of the king, and the others who are there at the court and whom the king always ends up by following. King Ahaz makes an inspection of his conduits to see if there will be enough water in case of a siege. In vain, says Isaiah, for "if you will not believe, you shall not continue" (*Is.* 7: 9b).

"Woe to the rebellious children," says the Lord,
  "who carry out a plan, but not mine;
and who make a league, but not of my spirit,
  that they may add sin to sin;
who set out to go down to Egypt,
without asking for my counsel,
to take refuge in the protection of Pharaoh,
  and to seek shelter in the shadow of Egypt!
Therefore shall the protection of Pharaoh turn to your shame,
  and the shelter in the shadow of Egypt to your humiliation.
(*Is.* 30: 1-3)

Jeremiah will have the same tone. "Who wishes to become a sage? Let him listen to me, Yahweh!" (cf. *Jer.* 8: 8-9; 9: 22-23). Let us remark in passing that it is from here that St. Paul took the theme, so dear to him, of I Corinthians, chapter 1, "Where is the sage . . . ."

The theme of the horse.

I am going to try to tell you, by means of a biblical "parable," what was at stake in this struggle.

The first time the horse was encountered was near Hazor in the north of Palestine, at the time when Joshua fought for conquest (*Jos.* 11). Armed with faith, he gained the victory. He won such a complete victory that he captured the chariots and horses. The horse was introduced into the Near East after the year 2000. The Israelites, with their backward civilization, in the thirteenth century before Christ had only their little gray donkeys. What should they do with the horses? The oracle of Yahweh was consulted, and they were told, "Cut their hamstrings." And so the horses were hamstrung.

But civilization came upon them rapidly. Some time later, under Solomon, large stables were built for the horses, and no king could be imagined as going out without being escorted by his cavalry. On the frontiers military posts with horses were set up, which were called "horse enclosures." The kings relied on horses!

Not always, however! An old psalm, Psalm 20, lets us listen to the prayer of a king — a good king, a king who is faithful to the covenant — who is sure of Yahweh:

> Now I know that the Lord will help his anointed; [3]
> he will answer him from his holy heaven
> with mighty victories by his right hand.

---

3. His anointed, "he who is rubbed with the oil of consecration," who is consecrated.

Some boast of chariots, and some of horses;
  but we boast of the name of the Lord our God.
They will collapse and fall;
  but we shall rise and stand upright.
Give victory to the king, O Lord;
  answer us when we call.

(*Ps.* 20: 6-9)

Well done! it is a moment of prayer. But in practice? In practice, as you have seen, horses are relied on. The horse is only a symbol of purely human support. But the prophets are there, guardians of the sacral tradition,[4] guardians of the faith.

See, in Hosea, the prayer which he puts in Israel's mouth (*Hos.* 14: 3):

Assyria shall not save us,
  we will not ride upon horses;
and we will say no more, "Our God,"
  to the work of our hands.

Idolatry, alliances, horses — all of these are interrelated. The horse is a symbol. Psalm 33, which belongs to the sacral tradition (after the great era, however), cries:

The war horse is a vain hope for victory,
  and by its great might it cannot save.
Behold, the eye of the Lord is on those who fear him.

(*Ps.* 33: 17-18)

Again, there is a series of directives to the king, which you can find in Deuteronomy, a levitical book which partakes of the sacral tradition: the king must be subject to the Levites, the king must "pray" every day in the Torah, the king must not have about

---

4. In my little book, *The Religion of Israel* (New York: Hawthorn Books, 1959, "The Twentieth Century Encyclopedia of Catholicism" series), I insisted that the prophets are "preservers," preservers of the sacral tradition of Israel.

him too many rich men, nor too many women (symbol of power), nor too many horses . . . . Here we are again: the horse, symbolic theme! (*Dt.* 17: 14-20).

Isaiah, finally, will say these things even better, in his splendid poem in chapter 2 (12-17):

For the Lord of hosts has a day
  against all that is proud and lofty,
  against all that is lifted up and high;
against all the cedars of Lebanon, lofty and lifted up;
  and against all the oaks of Bashan;
against all the high mountains,
  and against all the lofty hills;
against every high tower,
  and against every fortified wall;
against all the ships of Tarshish,[5]
  and against all the beautiful craft.
And the haughtiness of man shall be humbled,
  and the pride of men shall be brought low.

Such, therefore, are the sages: Yahwists "in the rough," I call them.

2. *Second stage*: *the Exile and the conversion of the sages.*

It is the Exile. Around the king (moreover, a king not too badly treated, seeing that we have found, at the foot of the tower of Ishtar at Babylon, tablets on which are represented gifts of sesame oil for him and his children), around the king there were officials, the whole remnant of the ruined state which had gone into captivity, the ones who are called the "princes" in the book of Jeremiah, royal princes, but also high officials, priests — the whole administration of the state.

In captivity, where no one had anything very important to

5. The ships which sail to Spain (the "ocean liners" of that age).

do, the priests devoted themselves to studying their traditions and the prophets to studying the vocation of Israel; the sages will listen to them, will become disciples of these Levites and these prophets: they will become converted. Their conversion is attested to by the first nine chapters of Proverbs. These chapters are full of borrowings from the books of pure sacral tradition, especially from Deuteronomy, which was completed during the Exile; from Jeremiah, who actually exercised his whole influence posthumously during the Exile; and, finally, from the Second Isaiah (chapters 40 to 55).

The sages had brought into exile all their treasures, all their wisdom: that old wisdom, so interesting with its detailed directives on good manners and morality, on politics and "religion" . . . . After the Exile, when they wanted to write an introduction to all that wisdom literature which they had saved, they fashioned a type of great "portico," very beautifully constructed in the prophetic "style," i.e., borrowed from the prophets and the Levites (chapters 1 to 9 of Proverbs). This is the *conversion of the sages*. This conversion which occurred during the Exile, will last.

How can I put it? The sages had become "100% Yahwists." They were no longer interested merely in their humanistic and international wisdom, which was their specialty, but in the history of Israel, in the hopes of Israel.

Without doubt, the most interesting of all these sages is Ben Sira (about 200 B.C.), because he is a "crossroads," because he is loquacious and tells all, both about international wisdom, but especially about the other wisdom, that of the covenant, Ben Sira gives us a "Sacred History" (ch. 44 ff.), especially a history of the priests, those priests who are so sublime, when they are seen through the figure of Simon, the high priest whom he knew. Simon is "his" high priest; he saw him come out of the temple, out of the veiled holy of holies, on the Day of Atonement, ready to impart the blessing to the assembled people.

The Temple is his center of interest, with the ceremonies

which are celebrated there and the priests who are met there. Close by he has his school. He says a prayer as he passes near the sanctuary (*Sir.* 51). He is able to compose psalms according to the rules. The sages were composers of psalms and were, without doubt, the editors of the Psalter: if there is any trace of the sacral tradition, it is certainly this, that Ben Sira starts to hope and places himself in the great current of messianic hope (*Sir.* 36).

3. *Third stage: the martyrdom of the sages.*

The conversion must have been complete, since many became martyrs under Antiochus IV Epiphanes. This was the first religious persecution, the first in which the Jews were attacked as servants of Yahweh, not as Jews (this is not a "racist" pogrom; it is a religious persecution). The Greek king, Antiochus IV Epiphanes, most likely had a statue of Zeus placed in the Temple; at any rate, he dared to put an altar to Zeus on the altar of holocausts. Then the altar of Yahweh ran with blood, was befouled, was made unclean. This was appalling, and these deeds, and similar ones, were the cause of the revolt of the Maccabees.

But, strangely enough, these events will be related by a sage, the one who wrote the book of Daniel (taking as his pseudonym the name of Daniel, which was an ancient name, a name of the Exile). It is, then, a sage who will describe to us with accuracy that religious revolt of the covenant people. And this revolt, do you know who is leading it? he asks us. Do you think that it is Maccabees? No! it is us, the sages! The sages have become the "committed intellectuals" in the service of the covenant. They will be the first martyrs of the covenant. This book of Daniel is, as it were, their "manifesto."

In chapter 11 of Daniel, a sage describes to us, in prophetic style, as if he were speaking of the future, the very events which he is living through at that moment. We are in 165 B.C., and the victory has not yet been won; it will not come for yet another year. At the present moment, there is a full-fledged persecution under an Antiochus who does not shrink from making martyrs. Let us hear the author:

> He [Antiochus] shall seduce with flattery those who violate the covenant; but the people who know their God shall stand firm and take action. And those among the people who are wise shall make many understand, though they shall fall by sword and flame, by captivity and plunder, for some days. When they fall, they shall receive a little help.[6] And many shall join themselves to them with flattery; and some of those who are wise shall fall, to refine and to cleanse them and to make them white, until the time of the end.
>
> (*Dn.* 11: 32-35)

If we go on to chapter 12: 3, we read that there will be a resurrection for the sake of the martyrs, and these martyrs were the sages! Sages, martyrs, risen from the dead! It is in the book of Daniel that we reach this splendid (and organic) development of the basic principles of the covenant. They will rise to share in the Kingdom of God at Jerusalem. The sages "shall shine like the brightness of the firmament; and those who turn many to righteousness,[7] like the stars for ever and ever" (*Dn.* 12: 3). The author, at the end of his book, places himself in the number of those who are candidates for resurrection. Yahweh says, "Go your way till the end; and you shall rest, and shall stand in your allotted place at the end of the days" (*Dn.* 12: 13).

We have thus finished surveying the journey of the sages. It will no doubt have made us fully appreciate, by a counterproof, what the faith of the Old Testament was.

---

6. This refers to the Maccabees, the people who use the sword and think they will accomplish much! But no! they will only provide a little help. It is we, the "committed intellectuals," the sages wish to assert, who are the true warriors.

7. This reminds us of the 'Teacher of Righteousness' who, perhaps at the same time, or a few dozen years later, will found the sect of Qumran.

SUGGESTED READINGS

Anderson, Bernhard, *Understanding the Old Testament,* Englewood Cliffs, New Jersey: Prentice-Hall, 1966, (Ch. 10).

Duesberg, Dom H., *Les scribes inspirés,* Paris, 1939, (2 vols.).

Dubarle, André Marie,, *Les Sages d'Israel,* Paris, 1947.

McKenzie, John, *The Two-Edged Sword,* Milwaukee: Bruce, 1956, (Ch. 12).

Robert, A., "Les attaches littéraires de Pr 1-9" in *Revue Biblique,* 1934-35.

CHAPTER 7:

The Biblical Man's Prayer

Let us take stock of what we have done to this point. We tried first of all to determine that situation of the biblical man: he is the image of God, situated between God, who he is not, and animals, over which he is lord; he is part of a people, a group; he is engaged in a covenant; he has a personal vocation, but one that exists for the good of the covenant.

How is the biblical man equipped in this situation? First of all, he has faith: it is the "upward gesture" of the biblical man — it receives all its vitality through a network of relations with God . . . . Prayer, which we shall discuss now, is the *breath of the biblical man,* who is a man before God in an attitude of dialogue, a dialogue which God inaugurates and permits.

As far as possible, I shall try, in brief compass, to get to the essence of prayer by considering biblical piety as found in the Psalter, which is by far its most wonderful expression. I said above that prayer is the breath of the biblical man: the collection of Psalms is given precisely this title in the Bible, the collection of *"tehilla"* ("breathing"). Tell me how you pray, and I will tell you what you are. Since this is so, it will be helpful to determine and describe the principal attitudes of prayer in the Psalter.

One more observation, before we begin. We must not lose sight of the fact that the Psalter is a "choice selection," since there were many more than just 150 psalms composed during this stage of the history of salvation. I think that the Church of Israel made this "choice selection" in exactly the same way as the Church of Jesus Christ made the "choice selection" of the Gospels. Let us not be surprised, therefore, to discover that these prayers are beautiful.

I ATTITUDES OF PRAYER IN THE PSALTER

1. *These attitudes of prayer are fundamental ones.*

The reason why the Church continues to use the Psalms is that she has seen in them the characteristics of such a lasting piety, a piety which so pierces through to the essentials, that pious souls can find in them a profoundly resonant chord. Two basic sentiments set the pattern of this prayer: adoration (*hallel*) and poverty (*anawa*).

a) *Hallel,* adoration.

The Psalter is a commentary on that magnificent passage from Isaiah which relates the inaugural vision, when Isaiah sank down in fear (= respect) before that God who makes men tremble and fascinates them at the same time. His fear is expressed in that triple *Sanctus* which he hears the seraphim singing. He experiences his insignificance, his deep uncleanliness, his sin before the Holy One, the "wholly other," the transcendent one. There is an abundance in the Bible of "these psalms of *hallel,* which correspond to the deepest and noblest need of all religion, which is to adore from the dust the one who is above us . . . . The poetic author of these hymns does not consider the events from the point of view of man, whom the waves raise up or dash down, but from the point of view of God, who can cast down or lift up according to his own good pleasure" (Gunkel).

The psalmist (cf. Psalm 150) wants the whole world, the old, the young, all races, the cosmos itself to join in praise, the rivers to clap their hands, and the mountains to sing for joy (listen to the mode of expression, which falters before the greatness of the task).

Let the sea roar, and all that fills it;
  the world and those who dwell in it!
Let the floods clap their hands;
  let the hills sing for joy together
before the Lord, for he comes to judge the earth.
(*Ps.* 98: 7-9)

This is the prayer which Berulle loved, the sentiment of selfless adoration which was so dear to Father Olier, the fundamental attitude . . . .

Let us listen again to Ben Sira, who, having tried to compose a psalm, gives us this advice:

When you praise the Lord, exalt him as much as you can;
  for he will surpass even that.
When you exalt him, put forth all your strength,
  and do not grow weary, for you cannot praise him enough.
(*Sir.* 43: 30)

b) *Anawa,* poverty.

The second fundamental attitude of prayer is *anawa,* a Hebrew word which we must know, because it is difficult to find an exact translation for it in English. *Anawa* is "poverty," but spiritual poverty, that to which we come as a result of a number of encounters with affliction and human weakness.

This "poverty" is sometimes expressed in dialogues, sometimes in monologues, in reproaches, which are often very free, very harsh, very angry, almost blasphemous. We are dealing (in Gide's expression) with the *"tutoyeurs"* of God, i.e., those on very familiar terms with him, who speak to God and challenge him passionately. Then, from that attitude, we pass on to silence, which is not exactly an oppressive silence, but, rather, the tranquil silence of the soul, of the deep inner self which begins to live again before God. Let us call this the prayer of "poverty," not the prayer of a beggar or a mendicant (it is that, but is even more than that), but the prayer of a soul which pours itself out before Yahweh, which expresses itself (sometimes with harshness) like Jeremiah in his "Confessions." [1] "O Lord, thou hast deceived me, and I was deceived .... Cursed be the day on which I was born" (*Jer.* 7: 14).

A psalm of this type, e.g., Psalm 88, seems to be pure despair:

O Lord, my God, I call for help by day;
  I cry out in the night before thee.
Let my prayer come before thee,
  incline thy ear to my cry!
For my soul is full of troubles,
  and my life draws near to Sheol.
I am reckoned among those who go down to the Pit;
  I am a man who has no strength,
like one forsaken among the dead,
  like the slain that lie in the grave,
like those whom thou dost remember no more,
  for they are cut off from thy hand.
Thou hast put me in the depths of the Pit,
  in the regions dark and deep ....
Thou hast caused my companions to shun me;
  thou hast made me a thing of horror to them.
I am shut in so that I cannot escape;
  my eye grows dim through sorrow.
Every day I call upon thee, O Lord;
  I spread out my hands to thee.
Dost thou work wonders for the dead?
  Do the shades rise up to praise thee? ...

---

1. Jeremiah was not, of course, the inventor of this literary form of "Confessions"; he used already extant liturgical lamentations. However, he integrated into this old form of the individual lamentation every bit of self it could bear: we hear a soul!

But I, O Lord, cry to thee,
  in the morning my prayer comes before thee.
O Lord, why dost thou cast me off?
  Why dost thou hide thy face from me?
Afflicted and close to death from my youth up,
  I suffer thy terrors; I am helpless.

Total despair? No! Never in the Bible: it is not possible, because there is belief in God. After these reproaches, these "blasphemies," there is silence(if not in this psalm, at least in general), the silence of Jeremiah, the silence of Job (ch. 42), and the silence of Psalm 131, that of the "child quieted at its mother's breast."

These are the two basic attitudes: adoration (complete theocentricism) and poverty (appeal to God).

2. *A great variety of prayer.*

In the Bible, we meet very diversified prayer (especially in the Psalter), which evokes extremely complex and diverse life situations, prayer which is "imbedded in life." It is to the credit of the great exegete Gunkel (1926) that he tried to pick out and catalog these "life situations" or typical circumstances which governed the composition of the psalms (the process of "literary forms," recommended by Pius XII,[2] applied to the psalms).[3]

---

2. The Second Vatican Council, in its Constitution on Divine Revelation, has also given its approval to the use of "literary forms" in interpreting Scripture. These are the words of the Fathers of the Council: "Those who search out the intention of the sacred writers must, among other things, have regard for literary forms. For truth is proposed and expressed in a variety of ways, depending on whether a text is history of one kind or another, or whether its form is that of prophecy, poetry, or some other type of speech. The interpreter must investigate what meaning the sacred writer intended to express and actually expressed in particular circumstances as he used contemporary literary forms in accordance with the situation of his own time and culture. For the correct understanding of what the sacred author wanted to assert, due attention must be paid to

We hear a multitude of people speaking in the Psalter. It is the huge crowd of the "poor": people in economic distress; exiles; Levites who are afraid of losing their place (the struggle among the "lower clergy" can be seen in a book like Chronicles, 300 B.C.); the accused (a score of psalms, cf. *Ps.* 22); prisoners, the ill,[4] illness being considered at that time a "proof" of Yahweh's punishment.

But side by side with these psalms of supplication are those which thank the Lord. Notice the attitude of thanksgiving suggested to the bridegroom: "Your wife will be like a fruitful vine within your house; your children will be like olive shoots around your table" (*Ps.* 128: 3).

The great national disasters, when Israel prays to Yahweh, find an echo in the Psalter (*Ps.* 74).

There are also pilgrimage psalms, which Jesus sang aloud while going up to Jerusalem at twelve years of age, psalms which glorify Jerusalem, Zion's "lieder."

Then there are the psalms in which the scholars expressed their experiences, the psalms which the sages composed (*Ps.* 73).

There are the *ex-voto* psalms, which were brought to the Temple; they were not engraved in stone as in Egypt, on a marble plaque, but were brought there to be sung.

What rich variety! The psalms must be studied in their variety; this is indispensable for an introduction to a prayer which

---

the customary and characteristic styles of perceiving, speaking, and narrating which prevailed at the time of the sacred writer, and to the customs men normally followed at that period in their everyday dealings with one another." (Translation from *The Documents of Vatican II,* New York: America Press et al., 1966.)

3. Today, a certain number of works are popularizing Gunkel's view among Catholics. A particularly interesting work is Drijvers, *The Psalms: Their Structure and Meaning* (New York: Herder and Herder, 1965).

4. Dom Duesberg has written a short work called *Le Psautier des malades.*

is "imbedded in life" and coincides with it — a prayer which, perhaps most of all, is a "universalizing" prayer.

3. *"Universalizing" prayer, because so varied.*

The Church gives us for prayer the psalms of prisoners, the accused, the "poor," at a time when I am happy and pretty much at peace. Is she not trying to invite me, at the suggestion of these psalms, to become a "brother to all," as Charles de Foucauld defined himself, to speak the language of others, to become a "speaker with tongues." Thus, the psalms are like suggestions or springboards for prayer.

It is immediately evident how a seemingly very critical way of approaching the psalms, i.e., Gunkel's attempt to determine the literary forms, is really very reverent; it introduces us to selfless or "universalizing" prayer, in which I lend my voice to others. I am invited by the Church to give an almost "stylized" expression — inspired in each case — to the cries, to the very passionate outbursts which I hear around myself, and which perhaps express in their indignant and spontaneous agitation a whole personal or collective drama. Consider, for example, the good woman who cries out, when she meets a priest, "If there were a good God, this would never happen" ("this" = war, injustice, etc.). I must transform these curses and this type of "blasphemy" into prayer, since the blood of Abel must be allowed to cry out (*Ps.* 88, 69, 109).

In reading these psalms, I correct in a Christian sense whatever violence there is in these "curses": a soul may cry out more strongly than usual at a moment when it seems as if God's "justice" ought to appear on the earth in a visible fashion. Now that we have the advantage of the total revelation concerning the afterlife, it is all the easier to pray these psalms in a "corrected" way.

One last example of these biblical prayers which seem so remote, yet are very contemporary: the apocalyptic psalms, the "great tumult" psalms, those which cry, "Yahweh is coming!

he is coming to judge the earth!" It is the fall of Jerusalem or the fall of Babylon or one of the other great events that man experiences. Remarkably enough, once we have lived these poems of the past, we hang on to them and we use them as our prayer, to call upon God at the great crises of history. There are psalms for that purpose (*Ps.* 74). But are there enough prayers today for the great events of history during which we live, as there were for the relatively insignificant events of the history of the past? This, then, is what the Church invites us to do by taking up these texts again in prayer; they are suggestions, and there is no doubt that the Bible (especially the Psalms) cannot be read except by one who is a bit of a symbolist or poet.[5]

We have, moreover, the example of Christ for this: Christ, whom St. Augustine calls "iste cantator psalmorum," that wonderful singer of the psalms, singer for each of us, singer for all mankind. Christ, singer of psalms! This role is easily understood when we consider the psalms of praise, and even the psalms of poverty, distress, and human misery: is he not the Poor One (*anaw*) par excellence? Did he not take full humanity upon himself ("non horruisti virginis uterum")?

But when the psalmists speak of their sins, can Christ sing those psalms? He is sinless! They will be, then, the sins of the Mystical Body; Christ says these psalms for us. He cannot call himself a sinner, but he can think of us, or, as St. Augustine says, "he speaks as the Head."

Thus, a true *apostolic prayer* can be found in the psalms.

No doubt more varied "degrees of wretchedness" can be found today than in biblical times (neither the Old Testament nor even the New Testament was acquainted with our cities with their

---

5. By this we mean that we must know how to read the texts on many planes and many levels and know how to transpose the typical situations into the concrete situations of today. If the reader is not a bit of a symbolist and poet, he has the opportunity to become such by turning frequently to the Bible.

great factories, the displacement of whole peoples, the wars of "democracy"). But the Bible says enough to the attentive heart about these things to suggest applications. Because all Israel was associated with this prayer, at least from the fourth century B.C. (when the Psalter became the choice selection, the single collection which was everyone's possession), it was for Israel truly an "introductory course" and an apprenticeship for apostolic prayer. All Israel felt more or less "burdened with others." If we are to busy ourselves about others (the task we must perform as educators), to mingle with them in their day-to-day life, must we not first have prayed for them in the secret places of our heart? How right the Church was to preserve the psalms for us!

4. *The "patina" of the prayer of the psalms.*

Since the prayer of the psalms belonged to successive generations, it has a certain progressive aspect to it and, in the language of cabinet makers, acquires a "patina." Since each generation has polished this piece of family furniture, we are struck by its glossy appearance.

Some psalms are very old. The tendency of contemporary critics is to push the date back farther than was previously accepted. One such critic, Albright, completely hypnotized by the *Ras-Shamra* documents, where he detects an abundance of concordances with the psalms, affirms that the majority of the psalms are very old. This is clearly an exaggeration. I do think, however, that, while there certainly are some pre-Exilic psalms, there are a great number of post-Exilic ones, too — at least half the Psalter. What preserves the "life" of many of the psalms is the fact that they have continued to be used over a period of ten centuries, not to speak of the past twenty centuries of Christianity and the centuries yet to come. Just imagine some French or English songs which would manage to "hang on" for over ten centuries!

How can we explain this vitality? It can only be explained

by the re-readings" done by generations very unlike one another in their outlook and their problems. A "re-reading" is always a work of the Church [6] and is a community action. It is an authoritative reading (since the Israelite community was always strongly governed and highly structured), a reading by the Church, which organically deepens the original meaning in proportion as the community raises itself up and becomes more spiritual. I would like to sketch out with you a "re-reading" of Psalm 47. Three "readings," three layers of meaning:

First Reading. This is the original reading, which I tend to assign to the tenth or ninth century before Christ. It deals with a festival at Zion. The ark of the covenant is about to be carried up to the Temple amid cries of joy, cries which are partly warlike and partly liturgical (after all, is not war a liturgy, a holy and religious action?).[7] All the people of Israel gather together in the court of the Temple after having accompanied the victorious ark. Psalm 47 is a hymn to Yahweh the King: God himself established his kingdom by putting together his nation again (the conquest was as yet unrealized at this time), by re-assembling his people.

Clap your hands, all peoples!
  Shout to God with loud songs of joy!
For the Lord, the Most High, is terrible,
  a great king over all the earth.
He subdued peoples under us,
  and nations under our feet.
He chose our heritage [8] for us,
  the pride of Jacob whom he loves.

---

6. We are considering Israel as an analogue of the Church.

7. The Bible sometimes mentions soldiers in sacred ornaments (is this the origin of the uniform?). There was no professional army at first; all Israel, a people of priests and a people of soldiers, rose up for Yahweh's battle.

8. This heritage is, in a word, Jerusalem.

God has gone up with a shout,
  the Lord with the sound of a trumpet.
Sing praises to God, sing praises!
  Sing praises to our King, sing praises!
For God is the king of all the earth;
  God sits on his holy throne.
The princes of the peoples gather
  as the people of the God of Abraham.[9]
For the shields [10] of the earth belong to God;
  he is highly exalted!

Second Reading. We are now in the fifth century B.C.; conquest is no longer on their minds. Long before, this was an integral part of their national folklore, but now they have no more than a large Holy City. It is around the time of Ezra and Nehemiah. Yet, this little people, reduced to nothing, this "Remnant" of the Babylonian Exile, has never before made such grandiose and pretentious claims. Claims, yes . . . but not for itself — for its God: this *conquered* God, who yet has *vctoriously* undergone the test of the Exile, reigns over the whole world. This, then, is what Israel claims for its God: universal kingship. My thoughts turn to Christ before Pilate, who had humiliated him, who had clothed him in derisive vesture, and who had led him forward crying, "Behold the Man"; it is at this very moment that Christ says, "I am a King!" It is precisely here that we see the constant paradox of the Bible: this little Israelite people (later on, Christ himself) which God has chosen, though so weak (*Infirma mundi elegit Deus*), in order that it might make strong claims for God alone, in order that it might better show forth the thoughts of God. This, then, is the "climate" of the second reading of Psalm 47.

In this psalm their longing for that universal kingdom is af-

9. Abraham came — poor, a wanderer — to Jerusalem in former times.

10. The shields = the leaders, the administrative "structure." They are also called the "spears" and the "angels" when they are on the attack.

firmed. It is at this time that verse 7b and 8a, which are not written in the same meter, were added (or, better, were "tacked on"):

> . . . . sing praises with a psalm!
> God reigns over the nations; . . .

Thus is reaffirmed the universal reign of God over the pagan nations, a reign which is pictured as a terrible one. Read those sumptuous visions of Isaiah, chapter 60:

> A multitude of camels shall cover you . . . .
> Foreigners shall build up your walls . . . .
> You shall suck the milk of nations,
> you shall suck the breast of kings.
>
> (*Is.* 60: 6, 10, 16)

Third Reading. We are at Alexandria. It is the reading of the Seventy, those rabbis who knew how to speak only Greek (although they still read Hebrew) and who translated, for the Jews of Alexandria,[11] the Bible (including of course, the Psalms). But there Jews are full of apologetic attitudes and universalistic aspirations; we are in a missionary era, when Judaism is addressing itself to the pagans and desiring to convert them. How will the Kingdom of God, of which the old psalm speaks, be understood now? It will be a kingdom brought into being by conversion; God does not desire to dominate the pagans but to convert them. This is why the Seventy will translate verse 10a, "The princes of the peoples are united *with the God* of Abraham." This is a modification of the meaning, which is in reality a deepening of meaning (in place of *am,* "people" [of the God of Abraham], they read *im,* "with" [the God of Abraham]).

The Kingdom of God has thus been kept at the center of interest in the psalm, in the course of the three readings, but it

11. The "ghetto" of Alexandria, if you will, but an open ghetto, concerned with religious conquest.

is a very limited Kingdom of God (first reading); a God who assembles his nation and his people; a God who dominates even the pagan lands (second reading); a God who dominates the universe by its conversion to him (third reading). And the whole world is invited to clap its hands!

This has been what I call a "patinaed" reading.

There will be even more "patinas" when Christ comes, who will pray and chant the psalms ("iste cantator psalmorum," that great chanter of psalms [12]), who will add his own reading to the various readings of his people:

Christ, at twelve years of age, goes up to Jerusalem, chanting, with fervor and enthusiasm, I imagine, Psalm 122 and all the other pilgrimage psalms.

Christ, during the sacred banquets, sings the *Hallel;* he carries on the tradition of his people, but, more than that, he fulfills it (the *Hallel* of the Last Supper: what a new tone it must have had!).

Christ on the cross, intones Psalm 22, then continues it in his heart: *Eli, Eli, lama sabachthani!* He will die with the words of Psalm 31 on his lips: "My Father, into thy hands I commit my *nephesh.*"

Do you see this "patina" and, in the case of Christ, the luster which the psalms have acquired? Christ is indeed the biblical man; he has caught all the tones and has orchestrated them to the full!

If we leave the Bible, we shall encounter all the Christian generations which have cast a patina on this prayer of the psalms. In the Middle Ages, for example, reading was taught through the psalms; *psalteratus* was a synonym of *litteratus* (St. Louis learned to read using the Latin Psalter). We could recall all those penitential psalms which were recited in groups of ten at the doors of the churches for sins committed, and those psalms

---

12. "*Iste*" does not have a pejorative tone, as often, but an admiring one.

of the dying recited at Cluny over the dying monks. Finally, we could see what we personally have wedged in the corners of our Psalter: those of its words which had been, at a given moment, our words, our entreaties.... We could recall (and why not?) the chants of our little country churches which "make David resound," as St. Jerome says. Perhaps the rhythm is wrong and the melody off tune, and yet is there not at times a touch of that ancient and everlasting poetry?

II THE "SACRAMENTS" OF GOD'S PRESENCE

The Psalter frequently makes mention of the "sacraments" of God's presence, those "signs of faith" of which we spoke above (chapter 6). Faith, in order to rise up to God, in its "upward gesture," must pass through some: "signs of faith," some traces of God, some "sacraments" of his presence.

The interior life of the psalmists is nourished by these signs. Contact is made with God:

— through the *Temple,* his dwelling-place, the place where he speaks.

— through the *community*. Read Psalm 133, that psalm which created monasteries and religious orders! "Behold, how good and pleasant it is when brothers dwell in unity!" (v. 1). There is also the recollection of those sacred banquets when "our heart is glad in Yahweh." [13] At the end of these meals, someone passed among the guests and put on their heads a kind of ointment (symbol of joy and of fecundity, which the heat of the head caused

---

13. "Our heart is glad in Yahweh" means to partake of a good meal during a religious festival. Cf. *Edent pauperes et saturabuntur,* or, again, *Biberunt et inebriati sunt nimis* (they drank and became exceedingly drunk!). Even during sacred meals they were far from being in perfect control of themselves!

to melt and trickle down). This joy of the little community at its reunion, an image of the larger community of Israel, "is like the precious oil upon the head, running down upon the beard, upon the beard of Aaron,[14] running down on the collar of his robes!" (*Ps.* 133). The community is indeed a spiritual place, the place of God's presence:

— through *history,* which is, after all, only the community extended in time, the community in process of becoming, where the believer, the "pious soul" finds God, that God who is involved in Israel's future and makes it evolve by his "mighty deeds."[15]

— through the *universe* as well. The psalmists find God in the universe. God is everywhere, God has care over everything. Psalm 104 is very typical; it is the "Canticle of the Creatures" of the Old Testament. What a breath of fresh air it is! It is easy to believe ourselves already in the climate of the Sermon on the Mount.

— through the *Torah*, finally, that privileged place above all for meeting God; it is his Word, these are his declarations.

Conclusion: *Prayer of Christ, Prayer of St. Paul.*

I have spoken enough of Christ praying the psalms to keep my conclusion brief. I will merely add a few reflections to emphasize the definitive note of the New Testament in this symphony of biblical prayer.

Christ gathers together and concentrates in himself all the best of biblical prayer. He is at home in the Psalter as if in his own garden. Prayer for him is the deepest breath of the biblical man; it is desire for God. It is the very expression of his sonship as well as its song. It is the lyric expression of the dogmatic definition which shows us Christ "*ad Patrem,*" turned toward the

---

14. The beard of Aaron was remembered as the longest one.

15. Yahweh = the God of "mighty deeds," who *is,* in the sense of the one who is "right in there."

Father, entirely directed to the Father. Prayer was the *basso ostinato* of his life; he prayed at all times (read the Gospel of St. Luke, which is the gospel of the prayer of Christ).

Let us pray *with him.* Note that St. Paul does not pray to Christ but prays to the Father, as Christ did, with Christ, as we also do at Mass. St. Paul praying with Christ to praise God for all that he has done — what a picture! Prayer of the heart, lyric prayer, which is like the expansion of his whole being in praise and selfless thanksgiving (see the beginning of Colossians and Ephesians). A true prayer of Catholic Action: Paul truly prayed with his life, put all his apostolic life into his prayer.

SUGGESTED READINGS

Anderson, Bernhard, *Understanding the Old Testament,* Englewood Cliffs, New Jersey: Prentice-Hall, 1966, (Ch. 15).

Bouyer, Louis, *The Meaning of Sacred Scripture,* Notre Dame, Ind.: Univ. of Notre Dame Press, 1958, (Ch. 12).

DeFraine, Jean, *Praying with the Bible,* New York: Desclee Co., 1964.

Drijvers, Pius, *The Psalms: Their Structure and Meaning,* New York: Herder and Herder, 1965.

Gelin, Albert, *The Psalms Are Our Prayers,* Collegeville, Minn: The Liturgical Press, 1964.

George, Augustin, *Praying the Psalms,* Notre Dame, Ind.: Fides Publishers, 1964.

Worden, Th., *The Psalms Are Christian Prayers,* New York: Sheed and Ward, 1961.

CHAPTER 8:

Sinful Man and His Restoration

To speak of sinful man's restoration will lead us back to the theme of the image and of Paradise, because sin was a negation of the grandeur of man, who, insofar as he was image of God, was placed between God, whom he did not equal, and the animals, which he ruled.

I SIN IN THE BIBLE [1]

We must trace our notion of sin to its roots in the Bible.

1. *Typical "case histories."*

To understand the concept of sin in the Bible, we must begin with some biblical "case histories"; they are paradigmatic

---

1. On this topic I would like to refer the reader to a book published by Desclee Company, *Sin in the Bible.* It contains an essay on sin in the Old Testament (Albert Gelin) and an essay on sin in the New Testament (Albert Descamps). In the latter essay the concept of sin in Hellenism and in a variety of religions is discussed in the light of the hypothesis that a true idea of sin can be arrived at in these religions. See also H. Rondet's *Pour une théologie du péché* (Lethielleux).

In the present treatment it is not possible for us to cover the whole subject; if this were our intention, we would have to study here, for example, the biblical notions of conversion and redemption. For studies on these subjects, we refer the reader to the work *Sin in the Bible,* mentioned above.

stories, stories which can be taken up by all men, since they are truly typical and full of meaning for us.

a) In first place among these "case histories" is that of the sin of Adam and Eve, the "protoplasts."

"Typical" sin it was, very well characterized by Genesis 3: 5-6, 22. It is the desire for knowledge of good and evil. Knowledge? Knowing in the Bible is a dynamic notion, which bespeaks at one and the same time an experience which is intimate, personal, and expressive of having power over someone or something. In this passage, granting the strangely moral climate of the whole chapter, we are aware of a power to decide between good and evil; there is a proud claim to moral autonomy. We cannot reproach Adam for having wished to become a kind of Prometheus, striving by his own power to become totally civilized; rather, he came to grief for having decided on his own what is good and what is evil *without referring to divine norms.* That last distinction is of supreme importance. Consider King Solomon (I *Kgs.* 3: 9), who asks God in his prayer, "Give thy servant therefore an understanding mind to govern thy people, that I may *discern between good and evil;* for who is able to govern this thy great people?" The reading of II Samuel 14: 17 completely confirms this idea, that the kings should decide between good and evil according to divine norms. The supreme decision from a moral point of view belongs to God.

In our consideration of the first sin, typical and exemplary par excellence, we see that it is a proud claim to moral autonomy; it is a form of *hybris* (arrogance).

Notice also that sin, according to the text of Genesis, is the *breaking of a personal relationship with God.* It supposes the experience of an exchange of dialogue, of a face to face confrontation. Adam tries to hide, and it is at that moment that he discovers, too late, the full gravity of his sin; God was his partner, and he broke the links which had united them: "Adam, where are you?"

Sin has a religious dimension. Let us not confuse this with some more or less morbid guilt feeling, as some are wont to do. It is not, for example, a kind of infantile guilt, touching us on the level of sexual tendencies. Sin in the Bible is a spiritual act and the taking of a spiritual position, a free breaking away from God.

Other important lessons in this text:

The sin of Adam and Eve was committed in the state of innocence and integrity. This means that the reason for man's ability to sin is not that he is a created being, a creature. There is no Gnostic savor in this biblical account; the human condition is not evil in itself. Created being is good, according to Genesis, and education is not fundamentally a disparagement of the creature. The sapiential books accept this as a given fact: man is educable.

Also, in this text, man is presented to us as victim. He is enveloped with instability and limited by it. Here we must recall once more the figure of the Serpent (*Nahash*); which represents a force outside humanity; Satan is present, and we must recognize his action when we read the Bible.

Finally, let us realize that sinful man was not left to his own devices. The promise of redemption was given immediately after the sin. As soon as he committed it, he entered into the dynamism of a ransom situation.

Thus, in Genesis 3, we have seen sin described in all its horror and in the light of all its moral religious implications.

b) I shall not delay long on the Tower of Babel episode; it is a question again of a sin of "arrogance" (*hybris*) (*Gn.* 11). I would ask you to read, immediately after the passage on the Fall (*Gn.* 3), the text of Ezekiel, chapter 28 and discover how much the latter depends on the former. The king of Tyre is situated in Paradise, or, rather, on the mountain of Paradise.[2] He lives there with a heavenly being, a "cherub." Then one day he commits an act of pride: he wishes to be like God. But God drives him away and places the cherub at the gate of Paradise to keep him from returning there. This is a very interesting symbolic re-enactment of the "historic" scene of the Fall (*Ez.* 28: 1-19).

c) The same lesson is taught in Isaiah, chapter 14, but this time the subject is the king of Babylon (*Is.* 14: 3-21, especially verses 13-15). This allows us to make an interesting observation: to get a clear picture of sin, we have chosen some case histories *outside* of Israel — Adam, the man of Babel, the king of Tyre, the king of Babylon, and (below, in the book of Daniel) Nebuchadnezzar. The authors of the Bible are universalists, and this quite naturally, they refer to Israel, to be sure, in these accounts taken from outside Israel; elsewhere they will also denounce sin proper to Israel. But the impression is inescapable that they are here denouncing sin in its very essence, as an attack on God at once transcendent and present to them. And this has a universal validity.

d) One last book, that of Daniel, will take up the same themes again. To begin with, there is the famous king Nebuchadnezzar (a typical king); he had "lifted up his heart," he has been brought low. Sin becomes a terrible attempted sacrilege against God, when Daniel (7: 24-27) presents to us, in apocalyptic language, Antiochus IV Epiphanes, that little "horn" (symbol of power) who rose up against God and persecuted his servants.

---

2. The mountain of Elohim, the mountain of the gods, which is located, according to Genesis, towards the north of the Fertile Crescent, on the spot where there are four rivers which seem to issue from the same single source. It corresponds to the Babylonian Olympus, which is located in the same area, in the mountains of the north. This is where the king of Tyre is situated.

2. *Sin enters the divine-human drama of the covenant.*

Sin assumes its full dimension only when it is placed in the context of the covenant.

The Bible, in these case histories, has denounced sin in its very essence.

Covenant, dialogue of God with humanity, its goal the Incarnation — this is the whole message of the Bible, this is all of religion. God wishes to be united with humanity (startling truth!). With marvelous pedagogy, he chose a witness-people and made a covenant with them. Bit by bit this covenant, which is community, which is conjugal union,[3] will develop by way of dialogue in proportion as Israel becomes a "qualitative" people and one spiritually more prepared for this communication (e.g., in Jeremiah's time). And one day, in order that this dialogue may be undertaken in depth, behold! here comes the Lord himself to take part in it, and — even better — to sum it up in his own person, since he is at the same time on our side and on God's side. The covenant will succeed, thanks to him.

a) *Sin as revolt against the rejection of God who is offering himself.*

In the light of the covenant, which we have just defined again, what is sin? It is the rupture of the bond of the covenant, it is the rejection of God who is offering himself, it is the refusal of dialogue. It is an attack on the heart of Yahweh (let us not forget that Yahweh is a God "of the bowels," of mercy and compassion); it is a rupture of the conjugal bond (*Ez.* 16, and especially *Jer.* 3, 4).

You have played the harlot with many lovers; . . .

---

3. Conjugal union is a concrete reality very appealing to our sensibilities but, at the same time, one which includes the concept of collaboration in a common work.

By the waysides you have sat awaiting lovers
like an Arab in the wilderness.
You have polluted the land
with your vile harlotry.

(*Jer*. 3: 1-2)

Sin is a denial of vocation. The word which expresses sin, the word (otherwise rare) which expresses the broken covenant, is *"pesha"* (rebellion). Read the very beautiful beginning of Isaiah (1: 2-4), where the redactor of the book has tried to place us fully into the spirit of Isaiah without delay:

Hear, O heavens, and give ear, O earth;
for the Lord has spoken:
"Sons have I reared and brought up,
but they have *rebelled* against me.
The ox knows its owner,
and the ass its master's crib;
but Israel does not *know,*
my people does not understand."
Ah, sinful nation,
a people laden with iniquity,
offspring of evildoers,
sons who deal corruptly!
They have forsaken the Lord,
they have despised the Holy One of Israel,
they are utterly estranged.

The text plays on the opposition of two words: *"pesha"* (rebellion) and *"yada"* (knowledge). What is this "knowledge" of God? It is the quasi-conjugal intimacy with God, communion with him (*"koinonia,"* St. Paul will say), a communion in faith, a religious bond. Discontinuing this knowledge, not wanting it any more, is "rebellion" (*pesha*).

b) *Aggressiveness and "positiveness" of sin.*

The above analysis makes us feel the tragic and irrational element of sin. It is an attack; it possesses what I shall call a characteristic "aggressiveness and positiveness," a positive charge of "hate" toward God. Exodus 20: 5-6 opposes, in succeeding verses, those who "love" God and those who "hate" him.

Positive aggressiveness shows forth in the fearful personifications which the Bible creates of sin, e.g., the personification in Genesis 4: 7, where sin is pictured like a ferocious beast which crouches at the door of Cain. Sin is also pictured as that wicked woman of the vision of Zechariah (5: 5-11); the passage speaks of rooting sin out of Israel. Sin is here personificed as a woman, a kind of impure goddess, like Astarte. She is put into a large hamper, with a cover of lead, and two other winged women will carry it to Shinar, to Babylon, the city of abominations where a house will be prepared for her. This is sin, very alive, very "fleshly," very positive. As far as sin's aggressiveness goes, this is also found in the psalms, in that frequent expression, the "mockers," the "scoffers," those who mock Yahweh, who laugh at Yahweh (cf. *Ps.* 1, "Blessed is the man who sits [not] in the seat of scoffers"). The expression will pass even into the Gospel, "Woe to you that laugh now" (*Lk.* 6: 25).

Do you wish to see this aggressiveness brought to its highest pitch? This will happen when sin becomes an aggression against the very person of Christ Jesus. "If I had not come . . . , they would not have sin" (*Jn.* 15: 22). It is clear why the Gospel is so hard on the sin against the Holy Spirit. It is because the sin against the Holy Spirit consists in not believing in the Son of Man. The Son of Man is precisely the one who is coming to fulfill God's covenant. This, then, is sin at its height, sin become unforgivable. It is, according to the vigorous expressions of the Epistle to the Hebrews, "to trample on the son of God," "to profane the blood of the covenant," "to outrage the Spirit of grace" (*Heb.* 10: 29-31). In reality it is saying "no" to the covenant, turning one's back on God who offers himself.

c) *Sin "disassembles" the People of God and divides the Church.*

Sin has thus thrust itself into the divine-human drama of the covenant. But, even though the covenant is an intimate relationship with God, let us not forget that it establishes a people, a partner-people of God, an Israel united before God. Sin destroys this very unity and "disassembles" Israel. All sin is a sin against Israel, since it lowers the spiritual level of Israel. All sin is a sin against the Church. The philosopher Paul Ricoeur has written strikingly on this topic: "Although the hidden criterion of morality is our relationship to God, the manifest and decisive criterion is our relationship to others."

It is very important to recognize that the Old Testament had already formulated in its own way, by concrete events, the words of the First Epistle of St. John, (4: 20): "If any one says, 'I love God,' and hates his brother, he is a liar; for he who does not love his brother [neighbor] whom he has seen, cannot love God whom he has not seen." In the Old Testament, already, *to know God is to love one's neighbor*. As proof of this, read the reproach of Jeremiah to King Jehoiakim (the prophets are very hard on the leaders, the rulers). This king leads his people into sin, and the prophet cries to him:

> Woe to him who builds his house by unrighteousness,
> and his upper rooms by injustice;
> who makes his neighbor serve him for nothing,
> and does not give him his wages;
> who says, "I will build myself a great house
> with spacious upper rooms,"
> and cuts out windows for it,
> paneling it with cedar,
> and painting it with vermilion.

Do you think you are a king
  because you compete in cedar?
Did not your father eat and drink
  and do justice and righteousness?
  Then it was well with him.
He judged the cause of the poor and needy;
  then it was well.
Is not this to *know me*?
  says the Lord.

(*Jer.* 22: 13-16)

It is clear, then, that one of the most profound phrases of the Old Testament, "to know God," means not only "to perform acts of worship," but also "to take up the cause of the unfortunate and poor."

d) *In the presence of sin, the "reflexes of the covenant" do not work any more.*

These are the reflexes which were triggered by certain key-words of the covenant: *hesed* (mercy), *emet* (faithfulness), *sedeq* (justice). The text of Hosea 2: 19-20 is a mosaic of these words which are the "reflexes of the covenant":

> I will betroth you to me for ever;[4] I will betroth you to me in righteousness and in *justice,* in steadfast love, and in *mercy.* I will betroth you to me in *faithfulness;* and you shall *know* the Lord.

Notice how the covenant is conducted:

"I will betroth you to me in *justice*": you will be like me, who am just, who create right and sanction it. Do what is right: I am just, be then just yourself.

"I will betroth you to me in steadfast love, and in *mercy.*"

4. Yahweh is speaking; Israel is the chosen people which does not "give in return," which is not faithful to the covenant. Yahweh will take the initiative to repair the covenant.

The Hebrew *hesed* implies affection, a mutual relationship which is, on God's part, mercy and tenderness, and, on man's part, love.

"I will betroth you to me in *faithfulness;* and you shall *know* the Lord." Knowledge of Yahweh: *yada.* Sin is its opposite: not to want to know, to rebel, *pesha.*

We could go on and on!

Because of these quasi-conjugal bonds which bind it to Yahweh, Israel is invited to a moral program of mutual "knowledge" and imitation; it must "cling to Yahweh," act like him. To sin is to desire no longer to imitate Yahweh (no longer to be faithful to the image), to free oneself from his great essential norms of conduct which we now recognize: *hesed* — goodness, compassion, bond of love, as of a father or a spouse (Latin *"pietas"*); *emet* — faithfulness, constancy (i.e., one can count on the other); *sedeq* — justice.

2. *Inventory of sin and oppressiveness of sin.*

a) We can begin the inventory of sin by citing some of the Bible's catalogs of sin. The Bible seems to have a predilection for catalogs of sins, a predilection for decalogues, but there are also sins listed in groups of three and six. For the computation by tens I refer the reader to the two decalogues which we possess, or, rather, the same decalogue, but twice recounted (*Ex.* 20 and *Dt.* 5). Psalm 15 also reckons by tens. Isaiah reckons by threes in chapter 33: 15. Ezekiel, chapter 18, perhaps reckons by twelves (dodecalogue).

These catalogs, in reality very necessary, come to us from a milieu shaped by Levites, who were the guardians of the sacral tradition; priests and Levites instruct Israel, even in the most minute details, how a rupture with Yahweh can take place.

But it is clear that the prophets insisted much more on the fact that sin is a concern of the "heart," of spiritual understanding, as we would say. To sin, for Hosea, is to strike at the heart of one's spouse. To sin, for Isaiah, is to level an attack on holiness, i.e., God's transcendence. For Jeremiah, who takes up Hosea again and "orchestrates" him, sin has its very root in the heart. This heart must be "circumcised," its "foreskin" must be cut off (a bold image: to enable the heart to accomplish its function, which is to know Yahweh). But Jeremiah writes at a time when there was a desire of restoration of man by God: God himself must circumcise the heart and make the necessary alterations (cf. Part II).

b) The oppressiveness of sin. The theme of the two cities, which runs through the whole Bible, illustrates this quite well. There is Jerusalem, and, opposite it, Sodom, Babel (Babylon). The frontiers of these two cities pass also (let us not forget it!) through our hearts; they pass through the middle of Israel. The Old Testament is not so "pharisaical" as to be unaware of this. Isaiah in his vivid first chapter hurls an extraordinary reproach:

> Hear the word of the Lord,
> you rulers of Sodom!
> Give ear to the teaching of our God,
> you people of Gomorrah!
>
> (*Is.* 1: 10)

Now, what is Sodom and Gomorrah, in the context? They are Jerusalem, which has become the "evil city," exactly like our hearts at times. The prophet continues, after having thundered against purely formalistic sacrifices:

> . . . learn to do good;
> seek justice,
> correct oppression;
> defend the fatherless,
> plead for the widow.
>
> (*Is.* 1: 17)

Do not think it remarkable that, in the Bible, the criterion of morality is always reference to our neighbor, our neighbor who must not be persecuted, must not be crushed down. Even when the prophet Nathan heaped reproaches on David for his sin, it was less for his having taken pleasure with Bethsheba, than for having taken the wife of his neighbor. The aspect of injustice is always the one most stressed in the Bible.[5]

The oppressiveness of sin again: the Bible clearly presents sin as a pressure, a hardening, a kind of "sin of the world," the world of Israel, an attitude which was adopted in the past, often through the oppressive authority of the leaders,[6] a spiritual attitude which is firmly established and hardened, which lies in the memory, is in the air which they breathe, and almost in the limbs of the body, like a permanent temptation. It is the result of a long history: a *collective sin-state,* a *sin of mutual responsibility.*

II THE RESTORATION OF MAN: THE INTERPLAY OF GRACE AND SIN

At a certain moment in Israel's history, immediately after the great prophetic period bearing the stamp of Hosea and Isaiah, an almost physical sensation of an inability to escape, of being made prisoner of that sin of hardening, is felt. That sin, which our forefathers had bequeathed to us, springs up again, summarized in the leaders. Jeremiah speaks of this sin-state, which clings to our skin (*Jer.* 13: 23):

---

5. The Bible and the Gospel do not polarize us toward sexuality, as some tend to think; justice towards one's neighbor is infinitely more important.

6. The leaders, those who bear responsibility, are treated very severely in the Bible: they aggravated the sin of the people. Elijah and Hosea are against the kings, Isaiah against the politicians (the sages). Jeremiah and Ezekiel are against the kings and against the Prophets of the Court.

Can the Ethiopian change his skin
  or the leopard his spots?
Then also you can do good
  who are accustomed to do evil.

This is the sin which covers over our hearts and which must be circumcised anew. Ezekiel paints a kind of fresco or composes a "bloody symphony," as Claudel would say: the blood of martyrs, the blood of injustices, the blood of sacrifices offered without conviction, the blood of the high places, the blood of women. The reader is breathless, as after the reading of the first three chapters of the Epistle to the Romans. Sin everywhere: sin of the pagans, sin of the Jews, no one is sinless. Sin is king! We could say that Paul exaggerates the picture to make us yearn for something else. This is just so: for Christ comes, comes as the new Adam, to redeem man.

But all this has been announced and prepared in the Old Testament, to take place precisely at that moment which was forechosen. It is the great turning point indicated by Jeremiah (31), Ezekiel (36), and Psalm 51 (*Miserere*).

1. *Jeremiah* 31 (to which Jeremiah 24 could be added). Yes, God will undertake to re-make our hearts, he will give us a "new heart." You have, through your own fault, caused the first covenant to fail; God will create a "new covenant." He will take you back again to zero and will forgive your sins. Here indeed is God's initiative, the grace which always precedes man's effort and makes it possible. Sin burrows itself into grace, as it were (like a worm into a piece of fruit), but sin is forgiven and will be consumed in its turn by grace. Better: sin will be opposed, will be restrained, will be "euchred" by a new grace.

Not only will the Lord take man back to zero by forgiving his sin, he will institute something new: he will write his law upon man's heart, and the law will become in him like a kind of interior instinct or interior light:

> Behold, the days are coming, says the Lord, when I will make a new covenant with the house of Israel and the house of Judah, not like the covenant which I made with their fathers when I took them by the hand to bring them out of the land of Egypt, my covenant which they broke, though I was their husband, says the Lord. But this is the covenant which I will make with the house of Israel after those days,[7] says the Lord: I will put my law within them, and I will write it upon their hearts; and I will be their God, and they shall be my people.[8] And no longer shall each man teach his neighbor and each his brother, saying, "Know the Lord," [9] for they shall all know me, for the least of them to the greatest, says the Lord; for I will forgive their iniquity, and I will remember their sin no more.
>
> (*Jer.* 31: 31-34)

2. *Ezekiel* 36. Ezekiel is a "professor" and very much accustomed to handling ideas. Less subject to the *"debar,"* which breaks in spontaneously, Ezekiel knows how to compose, how to make lists, how to keep accounts: he is a priest. He will tell us, then, in chapter 36, precisely what he is concerned about. He is concerned about a restoration of man. It is useful at this point, in reading Ezekiel 36, to keep Genesis 2: 7 in mind. There we have mention of the "breath of God" which establishes man in all his grandeur: man upright, steady on his feet, sure of himself, very much alive; but above all a human being who is moral, even holy. To ransom this being — what will this mean? Jeremiah answers: his heart will be re-made. Ezekiel will say: man must be

7. "Those days" – the days of 586 B.C., after that "black misery" of the siege which put an end to a certain period of the history of salvation.

8. The reader will recognize the formula of the covenant.

9. No more need of recourse to the priests, prophets, and sages to grasp the essence of religion (= knowledge).

re-made as in the beginning, by means of an infusion of *ruah,* of breath, of spirit.

> I will vindicate the holiness of my great name,[10] which has been profaned among the nations, and which you have profaned among them; and the nations will know that I am the Lord, says the Lord God, when through you I vindicate my holiness before their eyes. For I will take you from the nations, and gather you from all the countries, and bring you into your own land. I will sprinkle water [11] upon you, and you shall be clean from all your uncleannesses, and from all your idols I will cleanse you. A new heart I will give you, and a new spirit [12] I will put within you; and I will take out of your flesh the heart of stone [13] and give you a heart of flesh. And I will put my spirit [14] within you, and cause you to walk in my statutes and be careful to observe my ordinances.[15]
>
> (*Ez.* 36: 23-27)

---

10. I.e., I will show my power, my transcendence, by an intervention which will create the conditions of a new covenant.

11. This is a priest who is speaking; he uses liturgical images. Sin for him is a stain; he owes his vision of things to these priestly and ritual tendencies.

12. This new spirit will be like a "recharge" of your original spirit. As if the balance of flesh and spirit were inexact! Does this not seem to hint at that passage of Genesis 6: 3: God saw that man was only *basar,* only "flesh," and that he did not have enough *ruah,* "spirit," in him. Well then, God will breathe some into him!

13. The heart of stone is the one which "does not understand," which is heavy, weighed down, since the heart is the seat of understanding (cf. the adventure of Nabal, whose "heart died within him, and he became as a stone" I *Sm.* 25: 37). A heart of flesh is a penetrable, open, understanding heart.

14. I will re-enact the first creation for you.

15. God strives to make a new man, characterized by his moral constancy.

3. *Psalm* 51. The psalm *Miserere,* the deepest one of the Bible, has for its author a disciple of Ezekiel, who adopts the expressions of his master and draws applications from them. To predict that the messianic era will come, this is good; but to begin from this moment on to live a messianic life, this is better.

Psalm 51 begins with an analysis of sin, of sin in all its implications, the most profound analysis of sin which the Bible has preserved for us. The "poor one" who speaks is there, despondent, but turns to God and says to him: [16]

Purge me with hyssop, and I shall be clean;
wash me, and I shall be whiter than snow....
Create in me a clean heart, O God,
and put a new right spirit within me.[17]
Cast me not away from thy presence,
and take not thy holy spirit [18] from me.
Restore to me the joy of thy salvation,
and uphold me with a willing spirit....
(*Ps.* 51: 7, 10-12)

Yes, he is a "poor one," he is "worn out" ("a broken and contrite heart, O God, thou wilt not despise"). He cries to the Lord in order that he may bring about in him what he had promised through his prophet. Here we come face to face with

16. The expressions of Ezekiel will be easily recognized in this quotation: "Purge me," "create in me a clean heart," "spirit."

17. A "right spirit," because it is a question now of directing me, of making me a moral being.

18. Although the Revised Standard Version spells this word with a capital letter, Father Gelin feels that the correct interpretation requires it to be spelled with a small letter. He makes this comment accordingly: "'Thy holy spirit' = a holy inclination; you will work in me to make me holy (and I will work with you), and you will strive to lessen sin in me." *Trans.*

that transformation from a state of self-sufficiency to one of that poverty of spirit which is open to God and which obtains from him man's restoration. The one who prays is a man of fervent piety, but he is brought to see clearly that he can do nothing by himself alone; he utters a cry for grace. This is the transition from Pharisaism — the Pharisaism of the Israelites even in Ezekiel's time,[19] which consists in a certain confidence in one's own righteousness — to "publicanism," which is penetrable by God.

4. *St. Paul and the restoration of man by God.* It will be very profitable for the reader to re-read Psalm 51 together with what is perhaps the most beautiful passage in St. Paul (*Phil.* 3: 4 ff.):

> If any other man thinks he has reason for confidence in the flesh, I have more . . . . [I, who am] of the people of Israel . . . as to zeal a persecutor of the church, as to righteousness under the law blameless.
>
> (*Phil* 3: 4-6)

At heart this Paul, full of self-confidence, is a perfect Pharisee: he has wrought his own righteousness, his own holiness! Then comes his encounter with Christ:

> But whatever gain I had, I counted as loss for the sake of Christ. Indeed I count everything as loss because of the surpassing worth of knowing Christ Jesus my Lord.[20] For his sake I have suffered the loss of all things, and count them as refuse, in order that I may gain Christ and be found in

19. "Get yourselves a new heart," said the Ezekiel of the first style (18:31). And the Ezekiel of the second will cry out, "I, Yahweh, will make you a new heart!"

20. "To know Christ Jesus." All Christianity is contained in this formula, as we have seen the whole covenant is contained in the words "to know Yahweh."

> him,[21] not having a righteousness of my own, based on law, but that which is through faith in Christ, the righteousness from God that depends on faith.
>
> (*Phil.* 3: 7-9)

Faith as a basis, the opening to God and to Christ, the "void" which fills up! It is precisely here that the transition from Paul's Pharisaism to his publicanism is situated — in his poverty. This poverty is God's riches; in this poverty, God activates his spirit, God re-creates man. In this interplay of grace and sin, "grace abounded all the more" (*Rom.* 5: 20) — it has the last word and the victory.

21. "In him" = in Christ, in communion with him (*koinonia*).

SUGGESTED READINGS

Dubarle, André Marie, *The Biblical Doctrine of Original Sin,* London: Chapman, 1964. (Distributed in the United States by Herder and Herder, New York.)

Gelin, Albert, *The Key Concepts of the Old Testament,* New York: Sheed and Ward, 1955.

Guillet, Jacques, *Themes of the Bible,* Notre Dame, Ind.: Fides Publishers, 1960, (Ch. 2, 3, 4).

Schoonenberg, Piet, *Man and Sin,* Notre Dame, Ind.: Univ. of Notre Dame Press, 1965.

Van Imschoot, Paul, *Theology of the Old Testament,* Vol. I: God, New York: Desclee Co., 1954, (Part IV).

CHAPTER 9:

The New Adam - St. Paul's Teaching

The person of Adam is linked by the Bible with the whole of salvation history, of which Adam is, as it were, a rough draft. But Adam will not receive his whole value if he is looked upon only as a beginning; he is a normative "type," one who presents to us as already realized in himself that which the Lord looks forward to in all of us: to be truly his image. He is a normative "type" also in another sense, which St. Paul will reveal to us. St. Paul will be the one to tell us clearly that the first Adam was the "type" of the new Adam. Christ Jesus is the "type" of the perfect biblical man: there is only one biblical man — Christ. Adam is only an imperfect "type" of Christ. Let us, therefore, study the message bequeathed by St. Paul. However, since this original theologian is a genius at assimilation, being aware, as he was, of all the currents and vibrations of the religious worlds in which he was formed and re-formed,[1] it will be useful for us to reflect first on what probably prepared the way for this doctrine of the two Adams in Paul's thought.

I THE ANTECEDENTS OF THE DOCTRINE OF THE NEW ADAM

1. *Attention paid to Adam in apocalyptic circles.*

---

1. St. Paul is at the same time one who echoed the past and pointed to the future.

The apocalyptic circles reflected a good deal on Adam. Now, it is precisely in these circles that Paul was formed. His theology, insofar as it can be distilled from his writings, is an "apocalyptic" theology. The apocalyptic circles studied the sin of Adam; this was one of their main concerns. They reaffirmed, sometimes in rather pathetic terms, a link between the sin of the first father and the spiritual condition of humanity. For them, Adam is an example, a bad example: we find ourselves easily carried away by that evil instinct which is in us and to which the first man yielded, since, as the rabbis say, there was an evil instinct in Adam before his sin. He it was who brought about the entrance of death into this world.

Here is a very characteristic text on Adam's influence, taken from the Apocalypse of Esdras:[2] "If Adam, the first man, sinned and brought death upon all unseasonably, nevertheless, even among those who have been born of him, each one prepares his own future punishment and each one chooses for himself his future glory." Consequently, Adam was responsible only for his own soul's destiny; as for us, each of us is Adam for himself in his own turn.

There is here a clear doctrinal stand: Adam precipitated man into a cascade of misfortunes by the fact that he sinned, that he is an exemplar, and that, by his sin, mankind finds itself weakened. These misfortunes are principally death, and other evils which are enumerated, e.g., no longer does everyone speak Hebrew as in the beginning, our range of knowledge is more limited than in the beginning, etc. Basically, there is nothing more here than Genesis says.

---

2. The so-called Apocalypse of Esdras (Fourth Book of Esdras) is a Jewish apocalypse well known in Christianity. It is even printed at the end of the Latin Bible. A certain number of Christian liturgical texts have been taken from it, e.g., the Introit of the Mass for the Dead, *Requiem aeternam*. The themes of this apocalypse were current about the beginning of the Christian era (40-50 A.D.); they were put in writing later, probably at the same time as the Apocalypse of St. John.

Another apocalypse of that time, that of Baruch, takes the same approach. We can say, therefore, that there was special attention directed toward Adam in the apocalyptic circles at the time when Paul was writing; in particular, they focused on clarification of and reflection on Adam's sin. Yet, it must be noted that the mystery of evil is touched upon here only superficially and that the doctrine of sin is not entirely in accord with our Catholic dogma on original sin, as we have understood it since St. Paul. According to these apocalypses, each one must "play his own cards." "Every man is Adam for himself." Adam is only an alluring exemplar and a cause of weakness for mankind.

2. *The idea of the "two Adams" in the speculation of Philo.*

Philo was a Jewish scholar of the "Diaspora" who lived at Alexandria before the year 40 of our era, i.e., during the time Jesus was at Nazareth. Philo speculated on the two accounts of Genesis. As an introduction to his thought, it is curious to recall that a scholar like Lecomte du Noüy (who obviously did not know biblical criticism) introduced us, in his book *L'Avenir de l'esprit,* to a distinction analogous to Philo's.

First, let us re-read the Bible. One of the earliest passages of Genesis (chapter 1, which we have attributed to source P, the priestly source) solemnly presents us with the creation of the whole world in a qualitative order, so that we are shown, at the end of the account, the birth of Adam and Eve as the pinnacle of creation, its apogee: creation's king is introduced last. He is presented to us as image of God, between God, with whom he is not identical, and the animals, over whom he is lord. Then, a second account of creation, very psychological, but also very naive in some respects, depicts Adam for us, in chapter 2, as fashioned and molded by God, then as taking a wife (a woman drawn from his side). Our critical judgment is that this account belongs to source J, the Yahwist source, i.e., the first historical synthesis we have in the Bible.

Now let us consider Lecomte de Noüy's explanation of this passage. The "first Adam" (chapter 1) was only a rough draft; he was an inferior being created only with the instincts of procreation and self-preservation; he was not yet a man. The "second Adam" (chapter 2), on the other hand, to whom Yahweh gave a moral option, is a man who is capable of assuming responsibility, a true man.

Philo had already said something similar, but in an inverse sense. The "first Adam" (chapter 1) is man in God's image; the "second Adam" (chapter 2) is man made from the earth. The first is heavenly (*ouranios*) man, the second is earthly man. Elsewhere Philo modified his judgment somewhat. But we can see that we have here a theory on Adam which affirms that it is the heavenly man, the ideal man, a kind of "Platonic idea" of man, who was made first; and second, empirical man, less perfect, earthly, was created next as the father of men. Thus there is in Philo a "chronological" distance between the first, heavenly, man, and the second, earthly, man. Perhaps we shall be able to find something of this sort in St. Paul.

3. *Does the Old Testament present us with an eschatology of man?*

Does the Old Testament lead us to expect a person who is conceived of as an ideal representative of humanity, Man with a capital letter? It seems likely that at the time of St. Paul, the expression "Man" was a messianic designation.

Let us simply look at a text from St. Paul's time, that of Hebrews 2: 6 ff. You will recall how the author considers the famous Psalm 8: "What is man that thou art mindful of him, and the son of man that thou dost care for him? Yet thou hast made him little less than an 'elohim' . . . thou hast put all things under his feet" (especially the animals). In addition, you will recognize traces of Genesis 1: 26 here. This psalm is quoted in Hebrews, chapter 2, in order to apply it to Christ:

"What is man that thou art mindful of him,
or the son of man, that thou carest for him?
Thou didst make him *for a little while* lower than the angels,
thou hast crowned him with glory and honor,
putting everything in subjection under his feet."

Now in putting everything in subjection to him, he left nothing outside his control. As it is, we do not yet see everything in subjection to him. But we see Jesus, who for a little while was made lower than the angels, crowned with glory and honor because of the suffering of death, so that by the grace of God he might taste death for every one. For it was fitting that he, for whom and by whom all things exist, in bringing many sons to glory, should make the pioneer of their salvation perfect through suffering (*Heb.* 2: 6-10).

This is Jesus, Man par excellence. But in the Old Testament we also find this same title in a messianic sense. The Septuagint speaks of the coming of a man: "A star shall come forth out of Jacob, and *a man* shall rise out of Israel" (*Nm.* 24: 17).[3] "A man": messianic designation! Should this be connected with Genesis 1: 26-27? to Psalm 8? Are there not in Psalm 8, considered as a royal psalm, traces of a sense of expectation, viz., one day this Man, whom we are awaiting and who will be the perfect king of creation, will appear?

Certain of today's exegetes, e.g., Bentzen, think that the Son of Man of Daniel (7: 13) will be like a resurgence of the ancient figure of this lord of creation, lord especially of the animals. Was he not as well the conqueror of the beasts who symbolize the four empires? That figure, at the very least, is admirably adapted to become a personal messianic figure, and that interpretation was confirmed by Jesus, who called himself

---

3. The Greek text of the Septuagint actually reads "man" and not "scepter" as the Hebrew does. Cf. the Bible of Jerusalem, note i, p. 164.

the "Son of Man." Son of Man, a mysterious name which corresponds to the designation "Man" (with a capital letter): he will be a member of mankind, a son of Adam, who will realize, in a particularly outstanding way, what we have been waiting for since the creation of that Adam, the king of Paradise.

4. *The theme of the "two Adams" in the Synoptic tradition.*

Our last affirmation, and possibly the most practical: the theme of the "two Adams" was not invented by St. Paul; rather, we see it emerging clearly from the whole of the original Synoptic tradition.

Mark 1: 13 recalls that Jesus lived among the wild beasts, the same ones who obeyed Adam, according to the apocalypses. Living among wild beasts is a messianic trait (as well as a reference to the Paradise theme). Chapter 11 of Isaiah assures us that everything in the messianic age will be as in Paradise: the wild beasts will all be domesticated, they will all live in harmony with each other.

The wolf shall dwell with the lamb,
  and the leopard shall lie down with the kid,
and the calf and the lion and the fatling together,
  and a little child shall lead them.[4]
The cow and the bear shall feed;
  their young shall lie down together;
  and the lion shall eat straw like the ox.[5]
The sucking child shall play over the hole of the asp,
  and the weaned child shall put his hand on the
    adder's den.[6]

This is how Christ is portrayed in St. Mark: he is among

4. Man leads wild beasts = he domesticates them.

5. All animals will be herbivorous.

6. A return to the situation of the first Paradise: serpents will be feared no longer.

wild beasts, after a test from which — unlike Adam — he emerges victorious. Thus he inaugurates the new age, thus he victoriously re-enacts the adventure of the first man.

In St. Luke, it is worthy of note that the messianic temptation depicted in chapter 4 follows immediately after Jesus' genealogy, which ends thus: "Jesus . . . the son . . . of Joseph . . . the son of Adam, the son of God" (*Lk.* 3: 23-28). "The son of Adam, the son of God": this juxtaposition of the temptation and these names is extremely provocative. Father Lagrange says, "We must understand, from the preceding passage, that Jesus was a second Adam, much superior to the first." Perhaps St. Luke, who received so much from St. Paul, has in return given him something, i.e., not only a spirit of reconciliation, which is due to his very humanistic outlook, but also a certain primitive theological stance. Still, this possibility is by no means meant to minimize any originality contained in Paul's presentation of the new Adam, since Paul, in presenting Christ to us as the "new Adam," will not limit himself to the symbolic (and even somewhat mythological) ornamentation of victory over the wild animals.

II PRINCIPAL PAULINE TEXTS ON THE THEME OF THE NEW ADAM

1. *The First Epistle to the Corinthians* (15: 21-22, 45-49).

Before getting at the gist of this passage, let us try to point out its occasion. The occasion was a controversy about the resurrection, a controversy which arose from a very specific situation (the only type found in I Corinthians). Christianity at Corinth was very much affected, about 55 A.D., by the number of deaths which occurred. A certain number of practices were introduced and a certain mentality arose among the Corinthians following these deaths which were considered premature.

Some, remembering that baptism opened the door to the risen life, as St. Paul says (*Rom.* 6), received baptism in order to benefit the dead. Others, recalling that they were Greeks, and reasoning like the Athenians on the day Paul spoke to them about the resurrection of the dead (*Acts.* 17: 18), found difficulty, although they were Christians, in admitting the biblical idea of the resurrection: let there be talk of immortality — all well and good! — but not of resurrection.[7] Paul found himself facing their unrepentant Hellenism: "How can some of you say that there is no resurrection of the dead?" (I *Cor.* 15: 12). We can well enough imagine in the remarks of the Corinthians that note of lofty irony which we shall meet again among the Gnostics, the intellectuals. And we understand Paul's answer.

His reply consists in energetically affirming the total solidarity of the Christian with Christ. There is only one absolute value in the spiritual realm, and that is Christ Jesus. We are sharers of his destiny. His destiny is at once example and source; we must partake of it. Christianity is defined in terms of *"koinonia"* (communion); this is the reason why the formula *"in Christo"* suffices for Paul in designating the Christian's most intimate association conceivable — with Christ who gives life in the Spirit. Consequently, he must pass through where Christ has passed. Did he rise? Yes or no? This is the only important question, since it conditions everything: our faith and our destiny. This explains Paul's insistence in chapter 15: Christ has risen from the dead, we shall rise — if we rise, it is because Christ has risen. If we think that Christ has not risen, our faith is vain and empty (v. 14). If the fundamental fact of Easter is denied, there remains only a pretense of faith, a faith without content.

Chapter 15 is extremely important. Its concern is to reject

7. We recognize that Paul, while speaking to the Athenians of the resurrection of the dead, allowed himself to be called an "idle babbler." The idea of resurrection was very much opposed to the Platonic mentality of the Greeks.

vigorously a certain Platonic interpretation of our personal destiny, a certain pre-Gnostic mentality. Paul had seen the risen Christ in person; his witness and his teaching are not of less value than those of the other apostles. He saw him on the road to Damascus, and he experienced that extraordinary contact with the glorified Christ. He saw him, and to describe this vision he avails himself of some expressions current in Pharisaic tradition (which has some connection with the book of Daniel, chapter 12): the risen have a kind of body which is no longer of earthly quality (I *Cor.* 15: 35, 44).

But Paul bypasses this stage of a simple reply to specific difficulties in order to *broaden his vision into one great antithesis.* We should admire here Paul's twofold genius, historical and antithetical, harmoniously united. With him we never are left in a little, episodic idea; he promptly locates it in the framework of an elaborate historical vision, and, to integrate it better, he employs his antithetical, "professional" talent. And this is the Pauline structure which emerges.

Christ makes everything begin all over again, he renews everything; he is the great turning point of all history, the "once and for all" of the history of salvation. Mankind is on the way towards its destiny, and, along the way, it becomes attached to two men who bear its image. Let us understand clearly: an image which is not simply a diminished copy, but truly a force which derives from the original and can reproduce it. We bear in ourselves the image of earthly man and we bear in ourselves the image of heavenly man, like a transforming dynamism. We do not bear these two images, one superimposed upon the other, but we submit to the conquering dynamism of the stronger one. The first man, the second man: the first introduced death into the world; the second conquered death by his resurrection. Adam is by his nature unable to give us access to an "economy" of resurrection — that belongs to the second Adam. But let us read the text:

> For as by a man came death, by a man has come also the resurrection of the dead. For as in Adam all die, so also in Christ shall all be made alive (I *Cor.* 15: 21-22). Thus it is written [cf. *Gn.* 2: 7], "The first man Adam became a *living being* [*psyche*]"; the last Adam became a *life-giving spirit* [*pneuma*]. But it is not the spiritual which is first but the physical, and then the spiritual. The first man was from the earth, a man of dust [he is "muddy"]; the second man is from heaven. As was the man of dust, so are those who are of the dust; and as is the man of heaven, so are those who are of heaven. Just as we have borne the image of the man of dust, we shall also bear the image of the man of heaven.
>
> (I *Cor.* 15: 45-50)

Let us retrace this parallel more clearly: one man — another man; Adam — Christ; the first Adam — the last Adam; a "living being" — a "life-giving spirit." The first man, who belongs to the earth, who is of earthy substance, made of dirt, "muddy" — the second man, who belongs to the heavenly world; the first man, who has as his characteristic features flesh, blood, corruption, in a word, everything not suitable to a heavenly realm — the second, who is suited to this kingdom and who makes us fit for it. Thus this passage conveys in a remarkably concentrated manner the power which Christ has to transform his believers into his glorious body.

In summary, what are Paul's underlying purposes?

First of all, this parallelism corresponds to the innate tendency of Paul's preference for the universal. When the Jews awaited the Messiah, they hailed him as Son of David. So will he be, and Paul, who will tell the Romans that Christ Jesus "was descended from David according to the flesh" (*Rom.* 1: 3), knows this well. But, in speaking thus, there is a risk of presenting Jesus' work in too restrained a manner. In the world Jesus does not spring only from the little Jewish nation, he is not just the Son of

David. The Epistle to the Hebrews (perhaps dating from this epoch, since this epistle is one of the oldest ones) said that Christ is a replica of Melchizedek. Now, Melchizedek is a pagan; he lived before the theocratic and Levitical institution of Israel was organized; he was the representative of a human, natural priesthood. It is surprising to find coupled with Christ — over and above the Aaronic priesthood, over and above Israel — a pagan figure (albeit monotheistic). Paul does even better than this: besides David, besides Melchizedek, he links Christ with the first Adam, he traces him back to Adam. This is his way of indicating a theme of universality; there are two poles of mankind, Adam and the new Adam. Here, then, at one stroke, the traditional messianic titles are not abolished, but broadened and deepened, and Christ set in his unique place.

Paul's second purpose, accessory to the foregoing, perhaps is a polemic purpose directed against a Philo-type speculation. He takes aim — if not at Philo by name — at least at a similar outlook. You recall the speculative basis of the thought of the Jewish philosopher of Alexandria: there is the first Adam, the ideal Adam, image of God; then comes the empirical Adam, whose history we know of through chapters 2 and 3 of Genesis. Paul says, "It is not the spiritual which is first but the physical" (I *Cor.* 15: 46), i.e., the first, earthly Adam, the "muddy" Adam, and the second Adam, the spiritual Adam, the Adam who is the living image of God (*eikon*), Christ. He comes chronologically second, after some thousands of years [8] of the human history of salvation. Philo's speculation has returned in Paul's thought.

Paul's third purpose is to underscore the importance of the resurrection in this parallel: the new Adam is the *risen Adam*. It is precisely because he has risen that he has become the new Adam. From then on he belongs to the heavenly world, to which he can draw us. Verse 47, "The second man is from heaven," is

8. In the Bible's words, or the words of the French hymn, "After more than 4000 years . . . ."

not an allusion to the Incarnation. This verse must be read in the perspective of Romans 8: 11: "If the Spirit of him who raised Jesus from the dead dwells in you, he who raised Christ Jesus from the dead will give life to your mortal bodies also through his Spirit which dwells in you." The truth which St. Paul intends to emphasize is that the resurrection and the gift of the Spirit, which is linked with it, are sources of new life for mankind.

Paul's fourth purpose is a practical spiritual one. We shall not only bear the image of the heavenly Adam at the *Parousia,* but we can already, by anticipation, be people from on high, inhabitants of heaven. This is because the life of grace is already the glory of heaven; the *Parousia* will only be the revelation of that invisible but real state: "Just as we have borne the image of the man of dust, we shall also bear the image of the man of heaven."

These are, I believe, the four principal purposes of St. Paul: the purpose of setting Christ in his place, in an extraordinary universalism indicated by the title "Adam" — an accessory purpose of a polemic against Philo — the purpose of re-affirming that Christ is the life-giving *pneuma,* able to make us like himself as he is, i.e., risen — finally, a moral purpose, viz., to encourage us to live from this moment on in the state brought by the second Adam, to live in heaven.

2. *Epistle to the Romans* (5: 12-21).

The reader will recall that the occasion for the preceding text was a controversy over the resurrection, but, in speaking to us, Paul (who says everything at once, as St. John Chrysostom remarks) could not keep from touching indirectly upon the whole Christian economy. In Romans, chapter 5, this Christian economy is treated *ex professo,* in its fulness. Paul wishes to undertake a synthesis here, a vast and comprehensive synthesis. He has time for it; he is not pressed. The Second Epistle to the Corinthians remains to be written. He has three months at his disposal in Corinth. He is making plans for a trip (Acts tells us of this). He focuses on a doctrinal point: he will give us a panoramic tableau of the history of salvation, a tableau which is basically a meditation on Scripture. What is remarkable is that no single text emerges, because all Scripture has so become part of him. He knows it by heart and is able to extract from it the deep meaning of the history of salvation.

The Paul who gives us in Romans his *synthesis of soteriology,* his synthesis of the mystery of salvation, is indeed a genius.

> Therefore as sin came into the world through one man and death through sin, and so death spread to all men because all men sinned — sin indeed was in the world before the law was given, but sin is not counted where there is no law. Yet death reigned from Adam to Moses, even over those whose sins were not like the transgression of Adam, who was a type of the one who was to come.
>
> But the free gift is not like the trespass. For if many died through one man's trespass, much more have the grace of God and the free gift in the grace of that one man Jesus Christ abounded for many. And the free gift is not like the effect of that one man's sins. For the judgment following one trespass brought condemnation, but the free gift following many trespasses brings justification. If, because of one man's trespass, death reigned through that one man, much more will those who receive the abundance of grace and the free gift of righteousness reign in life through the one man Jesus Christ.
>
> Then as one man's trespass led to condemnation for all men, so one man's act of righteousness leads to acquittal and life for all men. For as by one man's disobedience many were made sinners, so by one man's obedience many will be made righteous.
>
> (*Rom.* 5: 12-19)

I do not wish to "peel off" each layer of the text, but simply to indicate its general direction:

It is concerned with comparing the two economies, the economy which I shall call "the economy of oppressiveness" and that which I shall call "the economy of liberation," Christ's economy. Both are characterized by an "ecumenical" solidarity and fecundity, that is to say, all the world partakes of them — but in opposing ways. The fecundity of Adam is, so to speak, the "fecundity" of sin (we might almost say "Sin"); we are present at the unleashing of the force "Sin," which is endowed with a kind of positive existence, as in the Old Testament. It is at work in mankind; there is a terrible burden which oppresses all men and which is initiated by the primordial sin of a single person, who mysteriously makes us all sharers in his sin: Sin originates in Adam.

Side by side with this, there is "the economy of liberation," in comparison with which the other was inversely typical. There, too, there is fecundity springing from a unique source, an "ecumenical" fecundity. But this parallelism is in reality a parallelism of superiority, because grace is a divine element, whereas sin was a diabolical one. There was a negative pole, and now mankind is positively polarized. The beginning of putting things to right was no doubt a good deal more difficult than the beginning of the downfall. But grace is brought by God; close by numerous sins, there is God at work in Christ.

This, then, is the remarkable antithetical genius of Paul, who wishes to arrange a tableau with as perfect a parallelism as possible: Adam the source — Christ the source. To assign to Adam his role of source, he did not investigate the origin of the force "Sin." He greatly simplified the notion of the "source," since Adam must be a perfectly contrasted "foil" to Christ; the shadow of Adam is on Christ, and the light of Christ by contrast illuminates the primitive figure of Adam. Still, I hope that I am not misunderstood: Paul knew well that Adam was not alone, that the devil was at work in his sin (cf. "Through the devil's envy death entered the world": *Wis.* 2: 24). There are also in Paul some allusions to the role of Eve (II *Cor.* 11: 3);

he knew well that she was there for some purpose.[9] He knows the devil's role, he knows Eve's role. But there is in his parallel some lack of awareness of those "pressures" which Adam felt; there is also something abrupt and automatic which emerges from the "literary genre" which Paul adopted: he wished to portray these two sources to us in vigorous contrast — unequally fecund, fecund in opposite senses, but fecund for the whole human race.

The second essential characteristic (rather, we should say existential characteristic) is the definition of the new Adam (always in contrast with the old Adam) by his attitude; this comes at the end of the tableau (*Rom.* 5: 19). The new Adam is defined by his obedience and is thereby opposed to the disobedience of his "type." Primitive Christianity unanimously saw in obedience the unchanging attitude of Christ from the moment of his entrance into the world (*Heb.* 10: 9). He came to obey. Hebrews 5: 8 is particularly suggestive in this sense: "Although he was a Son, he learned obedience through what he suffered." His mission was a mission of obedience; the fourth Gospel constantly repeats that Christ came to execute the orders of his Father. Christ's obedience at the Agony: "Not what I will, but what thou wilt" (*Mk.* 14: 36). Christ's obedience on the Cross: "When Jesus had received the vinegar, he said, 'It is finished' " (*Jn.* 19: 30).

Paul readily understood the obedience of Christ at its highest degree of perfection, namely, on the Cross (the text considered below will show this); the Cross is the highest expression of obedience, a moment when Christ manifested himself completely. We are aware of these moments in our lives. The occasions of heroism are not met every day, but there are moments when we give of ourselves and reveal our true selves. For St. Paul, the life of Christ is centered on that act of obedience of the

9. "From a woman sin had its beginning, and because of her we all die," says Ben Sira a bit ironically (*Sir.* 25: 24).

Cross. The life of Adam, in the light of Scripture, is centered on disobedience.

St. Paul, therefore, had two purposes: to emphasize and to illustrate by contrast the "ecumenical" fecundity of Christ, unique source of salvation — and then to insist on the fundamental orientation of his life in this world, a world brought back to unity by the act of the Cross, which is an act of obedience.

3. *Philippians* 2: 6-11.

This famous text is one which we almost know by heart. He "emptied himself, taking the form of a servant . . . humbled himself . . . . Therefore God has highly exalted him and bestowed on him the name which is above every name." It is Christ's epic: from heaven to humiliation, from humiliation to exaltation. Adam's epic can be discerned in filagree; it lies beneath Christ's. Adam, in contrast to Christ, wanted to raise himself up unlawfully, although he was only a man; consequently he was plunged into misfortunes. This is the point of view of St. Thomas and of Estius, that great exegete of the seventeenth century (slightly tainted with Jansenism), who has not become obsolete as a commentator of St. Paul.

What can we draw from this text? The process of self-glorification of the first Adam is opposed to the process of "poverty" of the second: he "emptied himself, taking the form of a servant." From being rich, he became "poor." This is the whole idea of *"anawa,"* the poverty of spirit, openness to God, and humility indicated in this passage. I am almost inclined to say that Paul's whole subconscious comes to the surface here. Was his life not a battle for humility against self-glorification? One phrase crops up again and again in his writings, "to glorify self"; he repeats it ceaselessly, "I must not glorify myself; I must be glorified in the Cross of Christ" (cf. *Gal.* 6: 14). We could say that it was an obsession with him, an obsession from which he wanted to free himself in anticipation of the great day: not to glorify self! He is giving witness to a drama . . . and to a victory, thanks to Christ!

III THE THEME OF THE "NEW MAN"

The theme of the new man is a concrete way of referring to human nature renewed by the influence of the life-giving Christ; we are conformed to the risen Christ, we are new men. Msgr. Cerfaux has put it very well: "The expression 'new man' is a transformation of the expression 'new Adam.'" Christ is nowhere referred to as the "new man" in St. Paul; the first time he is called that is in the letters of St. Ignatius of Antioch (not long after St. Paul, it is true). But, after all, Adam means "man." This theme of the "new man" is found in three spheres:

a) *The sacramental sphere.*

The "new man" is brought into being by baptism (*Rom.* 6: 3-11; *Gal.* 6: 15).

b) *The ethical sphere.*

The complete restoration of man is now assured, thanks to Christ; it consists in the messianic remolding of man, which was announced by the prophets, and which will consist in the infusion of a new heart, of a new spirit (Jeremiah - Ezekiel — Psalm 51). The influence of Christ will permeate the new man, or, rather, will bring it about that the image of God permeate the new man: "You have put off the old man with its practices and have put on the *new man, which is being renewed in knowledge after the image of its creator*" (*Col.* 3: 9-11).[10]

The essential thing is to bring the new man in us into

---

10. In this very rich text three major themes are recognizable: image, new man, and 'knowledge,' i.e., true religion.

alignment with Christ, who is in the process of transforming us. How? Colossians tells us, as does Ephesians: "But now put them all away: anger, wrath, malice, slander and foul talk from your mouth. Do not lie to one another, seeing that you have put off the old man with its practices and have put on the new man . . ." (*Col.* 3: 8-11).[11] This is the Christian program, the program of trying to make present in ourselves that Adam in God's image.

c) *The ecclesial sphere.*

Ephesians 2: 14 ff. presents this community aspect well: the two classes of mankind, Jews and pagans, forming a new collective Man.

This, then, is the whole program of radical restoration which is contained in the expressions "new Adam," "new man." The biblical man finds in Christ his model, his support, his fulfilment.

11. See also Ephesians 4: 22-24.

SUGGESTED READINGS

Brunot, Amédée, *St. Paul and His Message,* New York: Hawthorne, 1959. (Twentieth Century Encyclopedia of Catholicism.)

Cerfaux, Lucien, *Christ in the Theology of St. Paul,* New York: Herder and Herder, 1959.

New Testament Reading Guide, Collegeville, Minn.: The Liturgical Press, 1952. (Text and commentary on the Epistles of St. Paul, six pamphlets, 6-11.)

Prat, Fernand, *The Theology of St. Paul,* Westminster, Md.: Newman Press, 1958, (II, 171-179).

Tresmontant, Claude, *St. Paul and the Mystery of Christ,* New York: Harper, 1957.

Wikenhauser, Alfred, *Pauline Mysticism: Christ in the Mystical Teaching of St. Paul,* New York: Herder and Herder, 1960.

LEXICON OF HEBREW AND GREEK TERMS

HEBREW TERMS

Anawa: poverty, an aspect of faith; openness and abandonment to God. The opposite of self-sufficiency and confidence in one's own righteousness. **Anawim:** the "poor" (cf. the first beatitude). It is accompanied by openness to others; this is why the word **"anawa"** is translated by "humility" or "mildness" in Greek (Septuagint, Gospels).

Basar: flesh. No pejorative moral tone to this expression. It is merely the external or sensible manifestation of my deepest self (**nephesh**).

Batah: the spirit of trust which inclines one towards the God of the covenant (cf. the Latin **fiducia**).

Beraka: a concrete blessing – especially that of descendants, according to the etymology of the term.

Berit: bond of association, treaty.

Demut: resemblance, abstract term (cf. **selem**).

Dabar: the "Word" (of God) includes not only the intellectual and verbal expression of a reality, but also the reality itself, as a historical "deed." Dynamic word. Word-event. The best translation is sometimes "history" (**Jer.** 1: 1; **Lk.** 2: 10).

Emet: the faithfulness of God, solid foundation of the believer's security. God is faithful, true, and solid as the rock to which we cling. (**Emun** = the faithful one; **amen** = it is true, I affirm it.) The word defines the interior attitude of the covenant. Cf. **hesed.**

Gaal: to redeem a sacred value. Applied by the Second Isaiah to the redemption from Babylon. Cf. **pada.**

Hallel: adoration and praise before this daily fact: God exists and acts with power (in nature – in Israel's history).
Hallelu-yah: praise God!

Hakam (pl. **hakamim**): the "sage." Cf. **sopher.**

Hasidim: the "pious ones," the just of the Bible, those who live **hesed.**

Hesed: divine goodness and condescension. It is mercy, benevolence, but not meekness nor blind tenderness. Applied to man, it calls for a personal "consecration" to God, a return of love. Cf. **pietas.** It is the same relationship as that which defines the covenant. Cf. **emet.**

Ish: man; **ishsha** = woman, the feminine of **ish.**

Nahash: the Serpent . . . the same type of "monster" which the Babylonian gods conquered. Personification of evil.

Nedabim: the "volunteers" from among whom God will re-constitute the "little Remnant," the faithful and "qualitative" Israel.

Nephesh: the focal point of consciousness and of unity of the life-force. The living being, the living person, the "I." Cf. **basar** and **ruah.**

Ot: sensible sign of the presence and of the action of the transcendent God.

Pada: to redeem; applied in Deuteronomy to the redemption from Egypt, which led to the formation of the people of Israel. Cf. **gaal.**

Pesha: rejection of the covenant; rebellion against God; a spirit of aggressiveness inherent in sin.

Qum: to be standing, to rise up. (Hebrew term for resurrection.)

Ruah: the breath of the life process, the vital force which comes from God – which God breathes into man. The **nephesh** (human person) is not really alive unless God continually 'recharges' him with **ruah.** Since it comes from God, the **ruah** is also the source of the power and the activity displayed by man. The word has supernatural overtones.

Sedeq Yahweh: the justice of God – "his power of causing the moral order, prescribed by the conditions of the covenant, to be respected." More broadly: the salvific activity of God.

Selem: image, a very concrete representation (statue). Cf. **demut.**

Sheol: place into which the dead descend indistinctly and lead "a diminished life, without activity, almost without personality." Their **nephesh,** emptied and weakened, subsists at a slackened pace (these dead are called the **refaïm,** the "weak ones").

Sopher: the scribe (pl. **sopherim**).

Tannín: Dragon, one of a variety of primeval monsters (Leviathan, Rahab, Nahash).

Tehillah: breathing. The term used to describe the prayer of the biblical man. Hebrew title of the Psalter.

Yada: "knowledge" . . . not intellectual, but concrete, living, personal. It defines religion in its intimate aspect.

Zenut: (Greek **porneia**), used to refer to an illicit marriage union; implies certain impediments (impeding or diriment). The translation "fornication" is too severe.

GREEK TERMS

Agape: love, but in the sense of freely-given love, love which is a pure gift on the part of the one who loves.

Eikon: image, in the sense of a copy without any power to reproduce itself.

Eros: love, but in the sense of covetous-love, which denotes a lack, a need on the part of the one who loves.

Hybris: the arrogance which manifests itself in a man's wanting to make himself God by asserting an unjustifiable pretension.

Kairos: providential moment. In the Bible, it signifies the specific moment of God's intervention (cf. the "favorable time").

Morphe: image, in the sense of "form," of participation; more than a simple copy (**eikon**).

Porneia: fornication (cf. **zenut**).

Soma: body. In a Platonic setting, the body is usually pictured as the "tomb" of the soul, a play on the words "**soma**" (body) and "**sema**" (tomb).

Syntheke: treaty of alliance (cf. Latin **foedus**). **Diatheke** = Testament.